Where Is God in My Storm?

*Finding an Anchor
in Life's Rough Waters*

Where Is God in My Storm?

Finding an Anchor in Life's Rough Waters

by

Kenneth W. Hagin

15 14 13 12 11 10 09   07 06 05 04 03 02 01

Where Is God in My Storm?: Finding an Anchor in Life's Rough Waters
ISBN 13: 978-0-89276-751-9
ISBN 10: 0-89276-751-0

In the U.S. write:
Kenneth Hagin Ministries
P.O. Box 50126
Tulsa, OK 74150-0126
1-888-28-FAITH
www.rhema.org

In Canada write:
Kenneth Hagin Ministries
P.O. Box 335, Station D
Etobicoke (Toronto), Ontario
Canada, M9A 4X3
1-866-70-RHEMA
www.rhemacanada.org

CONTENTS

INTRODUCTION

In our day, people everywhere are searching for answers. Jesus told us that we would experience trouble in this world (John 16:33). But it seems that now more than ever, there is global confusion and unrest concerning the future.

What *does* the future hold? What is the significance of current world events? What about the future of our families? Are they going to be okay? Where can we turn for help? These are just some of the questions people are asking today.

Some have already given up hope. From their point of view, the answers they've been seeking so desperately are nowhere in sight. But the *real* answers to our questions can be found in God's Word. In fact, our success in life as individual believers is directly connected to the Word of God—how we value it and put it into practice in our daily lives.

This is especially true during stormy times. Jesus said in Matthew 7:24–25, *"Therefore whoever hears these sayings of Mine [God's Word], and does them, I will liken him to a wise man who built his house on the rock: and the rain descended, the floods came, and the winds blew and beat on that house; AND IT DID NOT FALL, for it was founded on the rock."*

If we want to triumph over the storms and rough waters of life, we must anchor our lives on the rock of God's Word. We must hear God's words and live by them. And we must remember that our Lord and Savior, Jesus Christ, has made a way for us to come through our storms to victory!

Chapter 1

WHEN STORMS RAGE
ON THE SEA OF LIFE

Have you ever noticed how two people can be faced with similar circumstances, yet each of them handles the situation differently? One person might panic and allow fear to overwhelm him, while the other person remains calm and focused on finding an answer or solution to the problem at hand.

This truth was never more clearly illustrated than on one particular night when Jesus and His disciples set sail on a ship across the Sea of Galilee.

MARK 4:35–38

35 On the same day, when evening had come, He said to them, "Let us cross over to the other side."

36 Now when they had left the multitude, they took Him along in the boat as He was. And other little boats were also with Him.

37 And a great windstorm arose, and the waves beat into the boat, so that it was already filling.

38 But He was in the stern, asleep on a pillow. And they awoke Him and said to Him, "Teacher, do You not care that we are perishing?"

Jesus was on the ship with the disciples. They were "all in the same boat," facing the same terrible circumstances. A storm had arisen, and huge waves were beating against the ship. The vessel was quickly filling with water.

This was no small test the disciples were facing. The *King James Version* calls this storm "*a great storm of wind.*" The *New International Version* says it was "*a furious squall.*" The men on that boat were experienced fishermen. I'm certain they had ridden out many a storm in their day. But this one was devastating, and on that night, they were afraid.

The disciples panicked during the storm—but Jesus was fast asleep! In a state of hysteria, the disciples woke Jesus up, exclaiming, "Don't You care that we're about to die!" But Jesus arose calmly and dealt effectively with the problem. Both Jesus and the disciples faced the same ordeal, yet they each handled the situation differently.

MARK 4:39–41

39 Then He [Jesus] arose and rebuked the wind, and said to the sea, "Peace, be still!" And the wind ceased and there was a great calm.

40 But He said to them, "Why are you so fearful? How is it that you have no faith?"

41 And they feared exceedingly, and said to one another, "Who can this be, that even the wind and the sea obey Him!"

There are several lessons we can learn from this story. The first lesson is, God never promised we would be free from troubles.

I wonder if the disciples had the mistaken idea that because Jesus was aboard the ship, there would automatically be smooth sailing. But notice Jesus did not prevent the storm from coming in the first place. Yet how many times have you heard people ask, "Why did God let this happen?"

No One Is Exempt From the Storms of Life

Tests and trials come to all of us. No one on the planet is exempt from these challenges. Jesus Himself told us that we would have tribulations or troubles.

JOHN 16:33

33 "These things I have spoken to you, that in Me you may have peace. In the world you will have tribulation; but be of good cheer, I have overcome the world."

Jesus didn't promise we would never encounter problems. In fact, Jesus plainly stated that we *would* have problems. Some ministers have given people the idea that as believers, we're never supposed to have any troubles. But that couldn't be further from the truth! We have a spiritual Enemy—Satan—and he is constantly testing us to find out whether we're up to the task of living according to what we say we believe.

Jesus told us we would have tribulation in this world. But He didn't stop there. He told us what to do in the midst of our troubles and tests: "Be of good cheer, for I have overcome the world!"

When Jesus came to the earth as a man, He resisted every temptation the Enemy could throw at Him. Living a sinless life, He withstood every evil onslaught, was willingly beaten and crucified, and defeated death, hell, and the grave! Jesus didn't "overcome the world" for Himself; He did it for you and me. Today, if we've accepted Jesus' great sacrifice, we have every reason to "be of good cheer" even in the midst of trouble and trials.

Entering the Ark of God's Safety and Rest

When Jesus and the disciples set sail, He had just finished teaching the multitude. He was no doubt tired, because we know that He went into the stern of the boat and lay down to sleep (Mark 4:36, 38). In this act, we see the limitations of humanity in the Savior. The human body can become exhausted and weak. It needs to be refreshed and recharged regularly.

But can you imagine sleeping on a boat in the middle of a fierce windstorm? I'm certain the little vessel was pitching and rolling with the crash of every swelling wave. I'm sure the night sky was brightly lit as flashes of lightning charged across the horizon. And the roaring of thunder could no doubt be heard from miles away.

Yet Jesus was asleep! And He must have been sleeping soundly, because the Bible says the disciples had to wake Him up.

In the Old Testament, a good night's sleep was considered a blessing from God to those who trusted completely in Him. David wrote in Psalm 4:8, *"I will both lie down in peace, and sleep; For You alone, O Lord, make me dwell in safety."*

In the same sense, believers under the New Covenant should be able to lie down and sleep peacefully and soundly—just as Jesus did on that ship—even if we're facing a test or trial. And when we awake, we should go through our day resting in the shelter of the Savior's arms.

When I talk about "resting" in the Lord, I'm not talking about literally sleeping or even lying down to rest. I'm talking about living in a state or condition of peace that passes your natural understanding (see Phil. 4:6–7). The storms of life may be raging, but when you're resting in the Lord, you have a sense of calm in your spirit that overrides what your senses, intellect, and emotions are screaming at you.

When you trust the Lord and rest in Him, you can remain calm in the midst of trouble. You know that you're safe and sound from the howling winds of adversity and destruction.

PROVERBS 3:5–6

5 Trust in the Lord with all your heart, And lean not on your own understanding;

6 In all your ways acknowledge Him, And He shall direct your paths.

If we want to enjoy peaceful sleep and enter into God's rest, we must put our trust in the Lord. In the midst of trouble, many people put their confidence in something else besides God. They might place their confidence in doctors or medical science, in financial institutions, in the economy, or even in their employment. Some put all of their trust in their pastor or a friend or family member. But we must ultimately put our faith and trust in the Lord.

God has blessed us with doctors and medical science, our job or vocations, and so forth. And we certainly need the support and encouragement of others who know how to believe God with us when we're facing adversity. But we must always remember that God is ultimately our source of supply. We must acknowledge Him gratefully for what He has done in our lives and for what He will do as we look to Him in faith and trust.

Clothed in humanity, Jesus knew the secret of placing His trust in His Father, and He lived it every day of His life. Yet as the disciples labored feverishly on that stormy night to keep their ship from sinking, they had no grasp of God's keeping power. And they failed to recognize Jesus' own confidence in God to protect and take care of Him.

In fact, the disciples mistook Jesus' "rest" as indifference. Apparently, they thought that since Jesus wasn't anxiously eyeing the storm, it meant that He didn't care about them. They asked, ". . .'Teacher, do You not care that we are perishing?'" (Mark 4:38). In modern language, what they said might sound something like this: "We could drown for all You care!"

Jesus' Authority Over Destruction

After the disciples awakened Jesus, He commanded the winds and the waves, "Peace! Be still!" In this act, we see Jesus exercising absolute authority over creation and over the Enemy's attempts to use nature to bring forth destruction.

In the beginning, Jesus was present with God in the creation of man. In Genesis 1:26, God said, ". . . 'Let Us make man in Our image, according to Our likeness. . . .'" So we know that Jesus was there when God formed man from the dust and breathed into him the "breath of life" (Gen. 2:7).

Jesus was also present with God in the beginning when God created the heavens and the earth (see John 1:1–5). That's why I believe when Jesus spoke to the sea in the midst of that terrible storm, the water recognized the voice of the Creator!

Jesus understood the forces of nature that opposed them that night on the Sea of Galilee. But He also understood the evil forces behind the storm, and He dealt with the situation accordingly. In Mark 1:23–25, we read that Jesus entered a synagogue and addressed an evil spirit that was present in a man, saying, ". . . *'Be quiet, and come out of him!'*" (v. 25). Then in Mark 4:39, He addressed a storm, saying, ". . . *'Peace, be still!'.* . ." Jesus understood that the devil was a force involved in the storm just as Satan was also involved in the oppression of the man in the synagogue.

"Yes," someone said, "Jesus could deal with those forces, because He was the Son of God."

Certainly, Jesus was fully God and fully man as He walked on the earth and died on the Cross. However, in His earthly ministry, even though He was the Son of God, Jesus operated as a man anointed by the Holy Ghost (Luke 4:18–19; Acts 10:38).

Jesus Delegated Authority to the Church

After Jesus' resurrection from the dead, He spoke to His followers concerning His authority, or power.

MATTHEW 28:18-20

18 And Jesus came and spoke to them, saying, "All authority has been given to Me in heaven and on earth.

19 Go therefore and make disciples of all the nations, baptizing them in the name of the Father and of the Son and of the Holy Spirit,

20 teaching them to observe all things that I have commanded you; and lo, I am with you always, even to the end of the age." Amen.

Jesus demonstrated His power and authority on the earth when He healed the sick, cast out demons, raised the dead, and commanded the elements to obey Him. And after His resurrection, He said, in effect, "I give My power to My Church."

That's talking about *you* if you've accepted Christ as your Savior. Jesus commanded His early Church, "Because all authority has been given to Me, I want you to go in My authority—in My Name—and make disciples." In the same way, He's saying to you and me today, "Go in the authority of My Name"! When you use your God-given authority against the Enemy of your soul, the devil recognizes that authority, and he *has* to obey!

We also need to understand that Satan is the god of this world.

2 CORINTHIANS 4:3-4 (KJV)

3 But if our gospel be hid, it is hid to them that are lost:

4 In whom THE GOD OF THIS WORLD [Satan] hath blinded the minds of them which believe not, lest the light of the glorious gospel of Christ, who is the image of God, should shine unto them.

Now, the Bible doesn't say that Satan is the god of those who have been born again. Although we live in this world, we are not of this world (John 17:15-16). Our true citizenship is in Heaven (Phil. 3:20). In this natural world, we encounter the natural. But if we're going to overcome in this world, we're going to have to reach into the spiritual realm and overcome through the power of Jesus Christ!

'Let's Go Over to the Other Side!'

There is a third lesson we can glean from Mark 4:35-41: Every word of Jesus is true and must be believed and obeyed.

In reading the passage in Mark chapter 4, we can sometimes overlook one very important phrase: "Let us cross over to the other side."

MARK 4:35
On the same day, when evening had come, He said to them, "LET US CROSS OVER TO THE OTHER SIDE."

Aparently, the disciples had overlooked this phrase too! Jesus, the Eternal Word of God, had declared ahead of time exactly where He and the disciples were headed: "to the other side" of the sea. Yet when contradictory circumstances arose in the form of a fierce windstorm, the disciples yielded to what their senses were telling them. And they forgot what the Word of God had said.

Jesus said concerning His Word, "'Heaven and earth shall pass away; but my words shall not pass away'" (Matt. 24:35; Mark 13:31; Luke 21:33). The Word of God is eternal. That means it is not subject to change.

When Jesus said, "Let's cross over to the other side," that's just what the Master intended to do. Had the disciples held fast to Jesus' words, they wouldn't have given place to panic and fear. I'm convinced that they could have calmed the storm themselves on the authority of Jesus' words. Instead, Jesus rebuked the storm, and the winds and the waves became calm. Then Jesus said to His disciples, ". . . 'Why are you so fearful? How is it that you have no faith?'" (v. 40).

Every one of us as believers is going to experience tests and troubles in life. The Enemy is going to challenge us to find out if we really believe what we claim to believe. You see, it's one thing to know that healing is the will of God and to be able to quote First Peter 2:24: ". . . by whose stripes you were healed." But it's another thing entirely to hold fast to your confession of faith when you're experiencing symptoms in your body or the doctor gives you a bad report.

When the waters are calm and the sky is peaceful and blue, it's easy to say, "I believe God's Word!" But when storms rage on the sea of life, what will do you do? Will you cry, "God! Why did You let this happen!" Or will you find shelter and peace in His arms? On the authority of God's unchanging Word, you can stand against the storms of life and see the raging winds of adversity cease. Not only can you experience peace in troubled times, you can "cross over to the other side" of those troubles and enjoy the victory God has in store for you!

Chapter 2

WHERE IS GOD IN TROUBLED TIMES?

In the last chapter, we looked at three lessons for our lives from Mark 4:35–41. Jesus was on a ship with the disciples when they encountered a fierce storm at sea. And He rebuked the winds and the waves, commanding, "Peace! Be still!"

But what happens when a storm is brewing on the sea of life, and by all appearances, God is nowhere to be found?

We can answer this with another instance in the Gospels. Jesus' disciples were at sea when a "great wind" arose (John 6:16–18). But this time, they were alone in the storm.

Jesus had just fed a multitude with one little boy's lunch. When the people saw the miracle, they exclaimed, ". . . *'This is truly the Prophet who is to come into the world'*" (John 6:14). Jesus knew that certain men were going to try to take Him by force and make Him king. So He retreated by Himself into a mountain, and His disciples set sail for Capernaum without Him.

JOHN 6:15–18

15 Therefore when Jesus perceived that they were about to come and take Him by force to make Him king, He departed again to the mountain by Himself alone.

16 Now when evening came, His disciples went down to the sea,

17 got into the boat, and went over the sea toward Capernaum. And it was already dark, and Jesus had not come to them.

18 Then the sea arose because a great wind was blowing.

Like the disciples, most of us have experienced natural storms in life. Perhaps we were safe inside our homes at the time. We may have seen the trees swaying in the wind and lightning flashing across the sky. Or perhaps we were driving in our vehicles and had to pull over to the side of road because the storm was so severe.

In recent years, many people in this country have experienced unimaginable devastation because of such natural disasters as Hurricane Katrina. And it seems we're hearing more and more reports from all over the world of similar incidences of massive destruction due to hurricanes, typhoons, and tsunamis.

Relatively few of us ever experience the kind of terrifying storms that get such widespread attention. But we've all experienced storms, personally. I'm talking about the storms of life. And sometimes those kinds of storms can be just as intense and devastating as the natural storms. During those times, no public official will declare a state of emergency in our lives. We probably won't receive disaster relief from the Red Cross. No men in uniform will come to our doorsteps to help us escape or get through the situation. But we are not helpless or alone! Jesus is with us, and He will help us navigate the stormy waters and reach our intended destination.

You Are Never Alone

In John chapter 6, the disciples were by all appearances alone as they faced a terrifying storm at sea. What can we learn from their situation that will help us weather and overcome our own storms of life?

The disciples were rowing against a strong wind that had caused the waters to grow rough. But it was also nighttime, which no doubt made the situation seem worse. Similarly, when we're faced with a troublesome challenge or storm, the rowing always gets rougher when darkness seems to hide the Presence of God.

Have you ever experienced a storm in your life when it seemed that the more you prayed, the darker things grew? You were rowing and rowing, yet seemed to be getting nowhere. You were in the middle of an ocean, so to speak, with no land in sight.

I think all of us at times have felt as if we couldn't hear God's voice or sense His Presence. Certainly, we had the assurance of our salvation. Yet during times like this when turmoil is all around us, it's easy to experience feelings of helplessness and confusion. Thoughts of giving up come against our minds. The Enemy tells us, "God is not going to come through for you this time." Darkness seems to fall like the night, and the rowing gets tough!

Have you ever prayed in the middle of a struggle and believed that God heard you—yet in time, you began to feel as if God had forgotten you? Although you knew it wasn't true, you felt as if your prayers had fallen on deaf ears. You kept sending out distress signals, but there was no evidence that your cries were being heard.

You probably already know the story of the luxury passenger liner *The Titanic* that sank in the Atlantic Ocean in 1912. More than 1,500 of its 2,223 passengers were lost that fateful night. On its maiden voyage from Southampton, England, to the New York harbor, the great ship collided with a huge iceberg near Newfoundland.

At that time, we didn't have the regulations in place that we do now concerning the number of lifeboats that must be present on vessels of that size. It is also now required that all ships maintain a 24-hour radio watch for distress signals. Had that particular law been instituted in 1912, hundreds of people onboard *The Titanic* could have been saved. History records that another ship less than 20 miles from *The Titanic* didn't recognize the distress signals because no dispatcher was on duty on the second ship!

There have been times when each one of us has felt that Heaven "was silent" when we prayed. We were distraught, yet help and hope seemed nowhere to be found. I'm sure the disciples wished Jesus had been present with them when they began to experience so much difficulty at sea.

Let's look at the rest of this passage in John chapter 6.

JOHN 6:19-21

19 So when they had rowed about three or four miles, THEY SAW JESUS walking on the sea and drawing near the boat; and they were afraid.

20 But He said to them, "It is I; do not be afraid."

21 Then they willingly received Him into the boat, and immediately the boat was at the land where they were going.

The disciples thought they were alone during that windstorm. Jesus had left them to go up onto the mountain. But now, all of a sudden, Jesus was near, walking toward them on the water. He could see them as they strained at the oars, yet they were unaware of His Presence. They were out in the water "about three or four miles" before they finally saw Him walking toward them as if on dry land.

Friend, you may be tempted to think God doesn't see your plight or problem. But He sees you. And if you're a Christian, He is not only with you, but He is also in you! He will not leave you, nor forsake you (Heb. 13:5). And He is forever watching over you, even when the rowing gets rough!

A Hand to Hold in the Darkness

When the storms of life rage and the darkness grows dense, that's no time to panic or fear. No matter how dark things seem, God can see what you can't see, and He promised to be with you and guide you safely to shore if you'll trust Him.

The psalmist David knew the truth that God is Light and the darkness can't hide anything from His view.

PSALM 139:12 (NIV)
12 Even the darkness will not be dark to you; the night will shine like the day, for DARKNESS IS AS LIGHT TO YOU.

Most of us have experienced a "midnight hour" in our lives—a time when things seemed their darkest and bleakest. That's probably how the disciples felt that night on the Sea of Galilee. It was nighttime, and they were struggling to no avail. The wind was blowing against them, and they were no doubt growing discouraged and weary. Yet it wasn't dark to the Master. He was watching over them with loving care. He is watching over us, too, and He promised to help us in our time of need.

ISAIAH 41:13 (KJV)

13 For I the Lord thy God will hold thy right hand, saying unto thee, Fear not; I will help thee.

God is always present with us, and we have His promise that He will help us. But when tests and trials come, the rowing always gets tougher when we allow our view of God to become masked by the storm. If we're not careful in the midst of a test or trial, we can lose our perspective of reality and take a wrong turn.

As a pastor, I always strongly caution people never to make a life-changing decision in the middle of a crisis. I counsel them to wait until they've had time to seek God and regain their composure and perspective.

I've seen people make life-changing decisions that they later regretted because they lost their perspective in a storm of life. Their ship was pitching and rolling on the waves of adversity, and they lost sight of the Master. They began to take matters into their own hands, and they suffered consequences that God never intended for them to suffer.

Storms have the ability to warp our perspective if we're not careful. Even some of the great men of the Bible temporarily lost their focus in times of trouble—a frustrated Moses as he dealt with a rebellious people; a heartsick David as he grieved for a son who had tried to kill him; a despondent Elijah as he ran from Jezebel; and an angered Jonah as God forgave a penitent nation. At times, duress and personal struggle caused the attitudes of these men to become tainted by their troubles. They wanted to give up and quit. They wanted to take matters into their own hands and try to change

God's plan. But God wanted them to cling to Him and let Him guide them through the storms and struggles.

That reminds me of a humorous story I once read about a little boy who awakened his parents one night in the middle of the night. He'd become afraid and wanted to climb into bed with Mom and Dad. Still half asleep, the father said, "Son, go back to bed. You're not alone; God is with you."

The little boy paused thoughtfully for a moment and answered, "I have an idea, Dad. Let's trade rooms. You go sleep with God and let me stay here with Mom."

Now, that's a funny anecdote, but it illustrates how we sometimes try to give God a "better idea" when things look dark and bleak, and answers seem long in coming. Instead, we simply need to hold on tightly to Jesus and trust Him to light our way until the darkness fades and the storm has passed.

It's so easy to lose your perspective of reality when things seem dark, but if you'll hold tightly to the Savior's hand, light will come. The day will dawn, and your "midnight hour" will be a thing of the past. Psalm 30:5 says, ". . . *Weeping may endure for a night, But joy comes in the morning.*"

Things Aren't Always as They Seem

Have you ever been away from home, and you woke up in the middle of the night disoriented? For just a few seconds you forgot where you were. I've had that experience, and it's a very strange feeling.

I recently heard a story about man who was staying with some friends, and he got up in the middle of the night to get a glass of water. As he was walking to the kitchen, something caught his attention in the darkness and he stopped, frozen with fear.

About four feet in front of him stood the image of a man. The houseguest made a move, and the other man moved too. Quickly, the man called out the name of the friend he was staying with. But there was no answer. Gathering all of his wits, he then leaped toward the image. A loud crashing sound woke up the entire house. The man had attacked his own image in a mirror.

So many times in a storm, things aren't as they seem. This was true for the disciples on the Sea of Galilee the night Jesus came walking toward them on the water. They thought they were fighting a storm on their own. They were doing the best they could using their own strength and expertise, yet success seemed to elude them.

But the disciples weren't really fighting the storm on their own that night. Jesus was closer than they realized. And I think in our lives today, instead of continuing to row and row against the current of the test or trial, it would often be a better idea to "stand still and see the salvation of God" (Exod. 14:13).

During times of trouble, some Christians wrestle with the "why" of their storm. Instead of rising up to contend for their victory and fight the good fight of faith (1 Tim. 6:12), they falter because they think that God is somehow against them. They haven't fully realized that they have an Enemy who's out to steal, kill, and destroy (John 10:10). And they haven't fully understood the unchanging truth that God is for them, not against them.

ROMANS 8:31

31 What then shall we say to these things? If God is for us, who can be against us?

In no way do I believe that God sends the storms of life or causes bad things to happen in the lives of His people. John 10:10 says it's the thief, the devil, who comes to steal, kill, and destroy. But it's during the tough times and the crises of life that we can experience the faithfulness of God—that He is for us, not against us.

In other words, it's easy to say, "God is faithful" because the Bible says that He's faithful. But when God reaches down and delivers us out of the dark, stormy waters of our tribulation, that's when we know for ourselves, *through experience*, that God is faithful!

ROMANS 5:3–4 (KJV)

3 . . . WE GLORY IN TRIBULATIONS also: knowing that tribulation worketh patience;

4 And patience, EXPERIENCE; and EXPERIENCE, hope . . .

A verse in the old hymn "The Solid Rock"[1] perfectly describes the confidence that comes from the experience of trusting God at all times.

Verse:

When darkness veils His lovely face,
I rest on His unchanging grace;
In every high and stormy gale,
My anchor holds within the veil.

Refrain:
On Christ, the solid Rock I stand;
All other ground is sinking sand,
All other ground is sinking sand.

Notice the writer said in this verse, "When darkness seems to hide His face, I rest on His unchanging grace. In every high and stormy gale, my anchor holds within the veil" (see Heb. 6:18–20). Those words convey a sense of calm and quiet confidence in God despite the howling, stormy winds of adversity that threatened his safety or well-being.

How to Hear From God in a Storm

Throughout the psalms that David wrote, he seemed to echo a solid confidence in God in times of chaos and fear. For example, in Psalm 46:10, David penned the words, *"Be still, and know that I am God. . . ."*

Sometimes we just need to be still and know that God is God! We need to take time to get quiet so we can hear His voice, especially when adversity threatens us or when we've experienced destruction in some area of our lives.

The prophet Elijah needed to hear the voice of God when Jezebel vowed to have him killed less than 24 hours after he had killed 400 prophets of Baal! The prophet ran for his life to Beersheba, where he curled up under a juniper tree and begged God to let him die.

1 KINGS 19:4

4 But he himself went a day's journey into the wilderness, and came and sat down under a broom tree. And he prayed that he might die, and said, "It is enough! Now, Lord, take my life, for I am no better than my fathers!"

Elijah had just accomplished a tremendous supernatural feat and a victory for the people of God who were still devoted to Him. But then he hit "rock bottom." Elijah thought his life was over and that he was all alone. However, the angel of the Lord appeared to Elijah, fed him supernaturally, and instructed him to go to Mount Horeb. It took Elijah 40 days to get there, but the food that Elijah had eaten from the angel's hand sustained him throughout the entire journey.

"Holed up" in a cave on Mount Horeb, the word of the Lord came to Elijah. God instructed him to stand outside and wait to hear what the Lord would say to His prophet. Elijah obeyed, and it says, *"And behold, the Lord passed by, and a great and strong wind tore into the mountains and broke the rocks in pieces before the Lord, BUT THE LORD WAS NOT IN THE WIND; and after the wind an earthquake, BUT THE LORD WAS NOT IN THE EARTHQUAKE . . ."* (1 Kings 19:11).

How many times do we look for God in something spectacular, such as the "wind and the earthquake," and miss Him in something less spectacular but equally supernatural? Perhaps Elijah felt the powerful effects of the wind and the earthquake and thought, *Surely, God is in this!* But the Bible says the Lord was not in the wind or the earthquake.

1 KINGS 19:12

12 . . . and after the earthquake a fire, but the Lord was not in the fire; and after the fire A STILL SMALL VOICE.

Often, believers weary themselves going from meeting to meeting, trying to find God in the "wind," the "earthquake," or the "fire." What they really need is to get quiet so they can hear the still, small voice of the Holy Spirit as He communicates to them within their own spirits.

Notice that after the fire, when things became quiet, Elijah heard the gentle whisper of God. Likewise, in the quietness of your times of meditation, you, too, can hear the voice of God. The thunder may roll, the lightning flash, and the winds of adversity howl. Waves on the sea of life may batter your ship until you think all hope is lost. But if you'll listen diligently to the Lord in the quiet times, you will hear His words of comfort, encouragement, and hope. And God will back up every one of those words with His mighty power and get you safely "to the other side"!

So how do you hear the voice of God in troubled times—in the midst of life's raging storms? I'll share with you a story that illustrates the importance of "being still" so you can hear the voice of God.

This story is set in a time before refrigerators were invented. It involves a young boy and an icehouse. Icehouses were usually built with thick walls, no windows, and tightly fitted doors. To keep certain perishable items cool, people obtained large blocks of ice during the winter and covered them with sawdust to prevent melting, allowing the ice to last well into summer. (This practice is why some people today call a refrigerator an *icebox*.)

One day a man lost his valuable watch while working in an icehouse. Raking through the layers of sawdust that covered the floor, the man and his fellow workers searched diligently for the valued timepiece, but without success. A small boy heard of the problem and slipped into the icehouse. Soon, he emerged from the cold with the man's watch. The men were amazed and asked the boy how he found it.

He said, "I closed the door, lay down in the sawdust, and kept very still. Soon, I heard the watch ticking. I didn't actually find the watch—the watch found *me!*"

In the clamor of adversity, we can get so caught up in what's happening around us that we can't tell whether God is there or not. Our view of Him is obscured by clouds of confusion and doubt. And the thoughts race so wildly through our minds that we can't hear His gentle but powerful voice. It's at times like these that we need to stop and get quiet before the Lord so He can "find" us! We need to be still before Him and be reminded that He is still God.

'Help Is Here—Do Not Be Afraid'

Frantically trying to reach Capernaum by ship that stormy night, the disciples couldn't see Jesus in the storm. They couldn't hear Him. They couldn't feel His Presence. Yet Jesus was watching over them. I want to encourage you today that no matter what storm you may be facing, your test or trial hasn't driven God away. He is an ever-present help in time of trouble (Ps. 46:1).

The disciples did finally see Jesus walking toward them on the water, and it says, ". . . *they were afraid*" (John 6:19). Immediately, Jesus said to them, ". . . '*It is I; do not be afraid*'" (v. 20).

The words "do not be afraid" are beautiful words when you feel helpless and trapped in some kind of problem. Think of the times you've heard stories about people getting trapped in places such as abandoned wells or collapsed mines. When help arrives, a rescue worker usually says something such as, "Help is here. Don't be afraid; we're going to get you out." Those are powerful words to the ears of someone who's been trapped alone in the darkness.

How much *more* powerful are those same words spoken by the Savior! When you're in the throes of adversity, you can hear the comforting words of Jesus: "Help is here. Don't be afraid; I'm going to rescue you and lead the way out."

Finally, John 6:21 says, "*Then they willingly received Him* [Jesus] *into the boat, and immediately the boat was at the land where they were going.*" When Jesus is on your ship, help is there! When you willingly receive His help by faith, trusting in Him, He will always get you to where you need to go—and He is always on time!

---

1 "The Solid Rock." Words, Edward Mote, circa 1834; music, William B. Bradbury, 1863.

Chapter 3

GOD WILL MAKE A WAY!

In times of adversity, we as believers often forget the many ways we've experienced God's power in the past. Instead, we tend to focus on the circumstances at hand and on what we can feel, hear, and see—what our natural senses tell us. We forget that there's an eternal, unseen realm that's more real than any substance or circumstance on this planet.

The same could certainly be said of God's people in Old Testament times. The Israelites saw countless demonstrations of the power of God. Yet time and time again, they doubted the Lord. They complained and rebelled against Him. God had promised to fight their battles for them, but they repeatedly doubted His Word.

Similarly, when we focus only on the circumstances that have us hemmed in, we're doubting God too. We're doubting His ability to protect us, deliver us, and meet our need.

Let's look at Deuteronomy chapter 1 and see what the Lord told the Israelites concerning His willingness to fight for them so they could enter the Promised Land. In this passage, God chastises His people for their lack of trust in Him.

DEUTERONOMY 1:29-33

29 "I said to you, 'Do not be terrified, or afraid of them.

30 The Lord your God, who goes before you, He will fight for you, according to all He did for you in Egypt before your eyes,

31 and in the wilderness where you saw how the Lord your God carried you, as a man carries his son, in all the way that you went until you came to this place.'

32 YET, FOR ALL THAT, YOU DID NOT BELIEVE THE LORD YOUR GOD,

33 who went in the way before you to search out a place for you to pitch your tents, to show you the way you should go, in the fire by night and in the cloud by day."

In verses 30 and 31, the Lord reminds His people of His great feats of power as He delivered them from Egypt's slavery and then protected them in the wilderness. He said, ". . . *you saw how the Lord your God carried you, as a man carries his son . . .*" (v. 31).

As I said previously, it doesn't matter what you may be going through—you are not alone. You have not been left helpless and hopeless. It doesn't matter how battle-weary you feel because of the challenges you're facing. If you will keep your faith and trust in the Lord, He will carry you "as a man carries his son." And God will make a way for you where there seems to be no way!

The truth is, God *has already* made a way for you! He accomplished it through Jesus' great act of redemption. Even when your problem looks impossible to solve, God has made a way where there seems to be no way (Isa. 43:19). In Christ, He has already gone before you and prepared a way of victory for you. Now you must walk out that victory by faith—walking closely with Him, hearing His voice, and obeying His Word.

Following in Jesus' Steps

I once read a story about a group of people stranded on a river bank with no visible means of crossing to the other side. As they were pondering their dilemma, one gentleman just began walking into the river. He got wet only up to his ankles as he walked straight across to the other side!

Amazed, the others followed suit, but when *they* entered the water, they began to slip and fall. They labored to swim across the river, and with great effort, they finally reached the opposite bank. Immediately, they began to inquire of the first man, "How did you do it?"

The man explained, "First, I spotted some old, sawed-off bridge piers just below the water's surface. I simply took a step of faith. One pier led to another, so I stepped from one pier to the next until I reached the other side."

We can learn a great lesson from this story. Wherever we need to go in life, God has already gone before us and prepared the way. If we'll simply follow Him, He will show us where the piers are! He will guide and guard every step, and we will safely reach our desired destination.

When I ran track in high school, I ran a particular race in which I became boxed in by three other runners as we neared the finish line. One runner was on my right, one was on my left, and the other runner was just one pace in front of me. I remember thinking, *I can't go right or left, so I can't go around this guy ahead of me. I could drop back, but I'd have to slow down, and I'm not going to do that. I'm going to keep my pace. But if this guy in front of me makes one misstep, we're both in big trouble!*

I was following the runner in front of me so closely that the second he picked a foot up off the ground, I was putting mine down in his place. And that's how closely we should be following Jesus! We need to be in perfect step with Him as He leads us, neither going ahead of Him nor falling behind. He has already been where we need to be. He knows the way. So we need to be diligent about staying in step with Him.

Have you ever followed someone through a wooded area who had been there before and was familiar with the lay of the land? That person knows where all the low branches and dense brush are located. If you follow his lead, you can maneuver that wooded path much more quickly and with greater ease. If you're really paying attention, when he moves left, you'll move left. When he moves right, you'll move right. And when he ducks, you'll duck!

Once during my term of service in the U.S. Army, we were conducting an exercise in a heavily wooded area. It was nighttime, and it was so dark out there in the woods, you could barely see your hand in front of your face. I remembered that one of the soldiers in our company had helped lay out the course, so I looked for that guy so I could team up with him.

I chose to follow this particular soldier because he had already gone before me, so to speak, and he knew the way! You can guess what happened. He and I made it through those woods faster than anyone else in the squadron. In fact, we had time to rest while we waited for everyone else to make it through!

God's Way Is Best

Most of us would readily acknowledge that God is all-knowing, all-powerful, and present everywhere, and that His wisdom far surpasses our own limited wisdom. Yet how many times do believers choose to go their own way—just as the children of Israel did—instead of following God's lead? Although God has promised His help, they go the more difficult way instead of going His way.

I'm not saying that following Jesus will always mean there will be "smooth sailing." But I am saying that Jesus' way will always be the right way. Jesus' way will be the way of peace, joy, strength, and ultimately, of great success and blessing.

Have you ever tried to do something your own way when you knew the Lord was leading you a different way? You made it through, but you felt exhausted afterward. You didn't sense the grace of God on your life, and you lost your joy. Hopefully, you learned a valuable lesson from your experience—that when you try to take the control of your life away from God, you can't do anything except fail! But even if you did learn the lesson, you learned it the hard way.

When I was three or four years old, my dad, Kenneth E. Hagin, pastored a church in Farmersville, Texas. Back in those days, many of the houses were called "shotgun" houses. There weren't any halls in those houses; each room was built right behind the other in single file. They were called shotgun houses because if you opened every door in the house, you could supposedly shoot a gun from the front door and the shot would pass through all the lined-up doors and out the back door!

We lived in a similar kind of house in Farmersville. The electricity in our house traveled through a wire that ran along the wall. In the living room, that wire ran right behind our couch. The way you turned on a light was to screw a light bulb into the socket attached to the wire. To turn off the light, you simply unscrewed the bulb.

One particular day, I was on the couch playing around that empty light socket, running my finger around the base of the opening. My dad cautioned me, "Son, stay away from that. It could shock you."

"Okay, Dad," I said. But just a few seconds later, I continued running my fingers around the rim of that socket. A minute or so later, suddenly—*bam*—my finger slipped off the rim, and the shock threw me backward off the couch and onto the floor!

I learned a valuable lesson through that experience. From that day forward, I never even got close to that light socket again! But I could have learned that lesson a much easier way. Instead, I learned it the hard way. It was not my father's will that I receive a painful electric shock. In fact, he had tried to prevent it by warning me about the potential danger. But I refused to listen.

In much the same way, God has made a way for you and me out of every test and trouble. And He will show us the way if we'll trust Him and obey His Word. Although we may think at times that we have a better way and a better plan, God's way is always best!

Will We Follow *God or* Refuse *Him?*

It was God's will that the Israelites enter the Promised Land and receive His highest and best blessings. And He was prepared to lead the way into that great land. He led them in the wilderness with a cloud by day and a pillar of fire by night. He took care of them, feeding and clothing them. He even provided riches for them as they left Egypt. And no one in the entire group was sick (see Ps. 105:37)! Yet an entire generation of people refused to cooperate with Him in possessing the land. After all He had done for them, they didn't trust that God had made a way!

In Numbers chapters 13 and 14, we can read about Moses' sending 12 spies into the land of Canaan, the Israelites' Promised Land. The spies were to bring back a report of the land. God had told His people that He had given them the land and that it was "...*flowing with milk and honey*..." (Exod. 3:8). However, when the spies returned to Moses, ten of the 12 men brought back an "evil report" of unbelief (Num. 13:32). They saw the giants in the land and said, in effect, "The land is indeed a land of milk and honey. But we were like grasshoppers in their sight. We're not able to take it!"

Only two of the spies—Joshua and Caleb—brought back a good report. In contrast to the other men, they said, "We are *well able* to take it!" (Num. 13:30).

In chapter 1 of this book, I talked about the fact that two people could encounter the same kind of challenge, yet receive two very different outcomes. That was definitely the case here. The unbelieving spies died in the wilderness, along with an entire generation of those who refused to believe. But Joshua and Caleb followed the Lord wholeheartedly. Older but still strong in faith, they were the only two men from that generation to enter the land 45 years later. They received the promise and possessed their inheritance because they believed God had given them the land, just as He said, and that He would make a way!

Our 'Promised Land' Today

What about us today? Through Christ's death, burial, and resurrection, God has provided us with everything we need in this life to walk in health, prosperity, spiritual freedom, and victory over the tests and trials that challenge us. This is our "promised land." God has already given it to us, and He has already prepared the way for us to walk in it. If that isn't enough, He also promises to help us enter in and possess these blessings! Will we *follow* Him or *refuse* Him?

If we choose to do what Joshua and Caleb did and believe what God has said and act on His Word, we will possess all the blessings of our "Promised Land." God has made a way for us—let's enter in and take the land!

Chapter 4

THE KEY TO POSSESSING PROMISES

Some people believe and teach that once you become a Christian, your battles and troubles are over, and you can just "coast" through life and live a life of ease. But that belief is unscriptural! As long as you're living and breathing on this planet, you are going to have to contend for the blessings God has given you. If you lie down and quit, the Enemy will have a heyday in your life.

"Yes," someone said, "but sometimes the battle is rough. It's not easy walking by faith all the time!" God has promised to help us and to lead the way. He did it for the Israelites, and a group of them finally did enter the land of promise. He will do the same for us today. The Bible says God is no respecter of persons (Acts 10:34); what He does for one, He will do for another. That means that what He did for His people under the Old Covenant, He will do for you and me today!

Each believer must come to the place where he either believes the Bible or he doesn't. I can prove from the Word of God and from experience that every word of God is pure, tried, and true. But what do *you* believe about God's Word?

Your believing affects your receiving. Unbelief prevented an entire generation of Israelites—everyone except two men—from entering the Promised Land. And unbelief can prevent you from entering *your* promised land and walking in God's highest and best.

On the other hand, faith in God caused a new generation of Israelites under Joshua's leadership to march in and possess their promised blessing! And God will do that same thing for you if you will trust Him.

Joshua and the believing generation of Israelites received what God intended—what God had already provided for them—and they did it by faith and obedience. Think about the many others in the Bible who received deliverance and blessing because they believed and obeyed God. Daniel was one of those people. He was delivered from the lions' den because of his faith in God and his obedience to Him.

Daniel was thrown into the lions' den because some of the king's officials were envious of Daniel's exalted position in the Babylonian kingdom. These men conspired against Daniel, manipulating King Darius into making a decree forbidding anyone to pray to anyone or anything else except the king for 30 days. Anyone caught disobeying this decree would be cast into a den of lions (see Dan. 6:1–9).

As soon as Daniel heard that the decree had been signed, the first thing he did was pray to God! And he didn't do it in secret!

DANIEL 6:10

10 Now when Daniel knew that the writing was signed, he went home. And in his upper room, with his windows open toward Jerusalem, he knelt down on his knees three times that day, and PRAYED AND GAVE THANKS BEFORE HIS GOD, as was his custom since early days.

When the men who had conspired against Daniel saw him praying, immediately they took the news straight to the king. The king was grieved and wished he had never signed the decree. He looked for a way to exempt Daniel, but legally, the king had no choice but to enforce the decree. So he ordered that Daniel be thrown to the lions (vv. 11–16).

We don't know exactly what happened in that den of lions. The scripture says the following about that remarkable night.

DANIEL 6:16–18

16 So the king gave the command, and they brought Daniel and cast him into the den of lions. But the king spoke, saying to Daniel, "Your God, whom you serve continually, He will deliver you."

17 Then a stone was brought and laid on the mouth of the den, and the king sealed it with his own signet ring and with the signets of his lords, that the purpose concerning Daniel might not be changed.

18 Now the king went to his palace and spent the night fasting; and no musicians were brought before him. Also his sleep went from him.

The following day, it says, "*The king arose very early in the morning and went in haste to the den of lions*" (v. 19).

'My God Is Able!'

It's interesting that when the king finally arrived at the lions' den the following morning, he cried out to Daniel: ". . . *'Daniel, servant of the living God, has your God, whom you serve continually, been able to deliver you from the lions?'*" (v. 20).

I don't know about you, but from a natural standpoint, I think it's a bit strange to throw someone into a den of ravenous lions and then go back to the scene 24 hours later and call the person by name! Could it be that this heathen king had faith that God would make a way for His loyal servant Daniel?

The king cried out with great passion, "Daniel, has your God, Whom you serve continually, been able to deliver you?"

And, you know the story. Daniel answered the king, saying, in effect, "Yes, O king! My God is able!" Then he reported to King Darius, *"My God sent His angel and shut the lions' mouths, so that they have not hurt me, because I was found innocent before Him; and also, O king, I have done no wrong before you"* (v. 22).

DANIEL 6:23

23 Now the king was exceedingly glad for him, and commanded that they should take Daniel up out of the den. So Daniel was taken up out of the den, and no injury whatever was found on him, BECAUSE HE BELIEVED IN HIS GOD.

When we read what happened in the lions' den that night, the Bible simply says that *". . . God sent His angel and shut the lions' mouths . . ."* (v. 22). We may not know all of the details of the story, but we do know that Daniel prevailed in the midst of trouble because "the God Whom he served continually" had made a way!

God performed an astounding miracle on Daniel's behalf. Those were not trained lions in that pit! They were wild beasts that would have torn Daniel to shreds if it were not for the saving, delivering power of God. We know that's true, because when the king found Daniel alive, he ordered that all those who had con-spired against him—along with their families—be thrown into the same den of lions. And it says that before those people even reached the floor of the den, their bones were crushed in the lions' jaws (Dan. 6:24).

Daniel's victory reveals to us the important truth that what-ever we believe in the midst of our test or trial will determine our outcome. We can either be "eaten up" by our problems, or we can believe that God will help us find a way to possess our promises.

No More Wishful Thinking

You may be standing right now at the very edge of your prom-ised land, looking longingly at the blessing you need or want. But if you don't believe that God has made a way and that He is lead-ing you to possess that land by faith, your spiritual enemies are going to prevent you from possessing your promise.

Instead of staring at the promised land in the distance, wish-ing you could break through and possess it, why not begin look-ing for your deliverance! Why don't you allow God to show you how your stumbling blocks can be turned into stepping-stones? Instead of bemoaning your situation, you can view it as another opportunity for God to show Himself strong on your behalf!

'Bow or Burn!'

Let's look at how Daniel's three friends used a "fiery" trial as an opportunity to prove the faithfulness of God in their own lives.

In the early days of their captivity in Babylon, Daniel and his three friends, Shadrach, Meshach, and Abednego, served in the palace of King Nebuchadnezzar. One day, Nebuchadnezzar decided to make a golden idol, and he issued a command that everyone in attendance at its dedication must worship the image when the music began to play. Whoever didn't bow immediately and worship was to be thrown into a fiery furnace.

At the dedication, certain men reported to the king that three of the king's own officials, Shadrach, Meshach, and Abednego, had not bowed to worship the idol. Furious, the king ordered that the three men be brought before him (see Dan. 3:1–13).

DANIEL 3:14–15

14 Nebuchadnezzar spoke, saying to them, "Is it true, Shadrach, Meshach, and Abed-Nego, that you do not serve my gods or worship the gold image which I have set up?

15 Now if you are ready at the time you hear the sound of the horn, flute, harp, lyre, and psaltery, in symphony with all kinds of music, and you fall down and worship the image which I have made, good! But if you do not worship, you shall be cast immediately into the midst of a burning fiery furnace. And who is the god who will deliver you from my hands?"

Even after the king gave these three Hebrew men a second chance to worship the image, Shadrach, Meshach, and Abednego refused to worship any god except the God of Israel (vv. 16–18). The king basically said to them, "Bow or burn!" But I want you to notice that they didn't do either! They didn't bow and they didn't burn because their God brought them through the fire victoriously!

DANIEL 3:19-27

19 Nebuchadnezzar was full of fury, and the expression on his face changed toward Shadrach, Meshach, and Abed-Nego. He spoke and commanded that they heat the furnace seven times more than it was usually heated.

20 And he commanded certain mighty men of valor who were in his army to bind Shadrach, Meshach, and Abed-Nego, and cast them into the burning fiery furnace.

21 Then these men were bound in their coats, their trousers, their turbans, and their other garments, and were cast into the midst of the burning fiery furnace.

22 Therefore, because the king's command was urgent, and the furnace exceedingly hot, the flame of the fire killed those men who took up Shadrach, Meshach, and Abed-Nego.

23 And these three men, Shadrach, Meshach, and Abed-Nego, fell down bound into the midst of the burning fiery furnace.

24 Then King Nebuchadnezzar was astonished; and he rose in haste and spoke, saying to his counselors, "Did we not cast three men bound into the midst of the fire?" They answered and said to the king, "True, O king."

25 "Look!" he answered, "I SEE FOUR MEN LOOSE, WALKING IN THE MIDST OF THE FIRE; AND THEY ARE NOT HURT, AND THE FORM OF THE FOURTH IS LIKE THE SON OF GOD."

26 Then Nebuchadnezzar went near the mouth of the burning fiery furnace and spoke, saying, "Shadrach, Meshach, and Abed-Nego, servants of the Most High God, come out, and come here." Then Shadrach, Meshach, and Abed-Nego came from the midst of the fire.

27 And the satraps, administrators, governors, and the king's counselors gathered together, and they saw these men ON

WHOSE BODIES THE FIRE HAD NO POWER; the hair of their head was not singed nor were their garments affected, and the smell of fire was not on them.

The Enemy constantly tries to threaten believers today, saying things such as, "If you trust God, you're going to be sorry. He's not going to come through for you, and, boy, are you going to look silly!" He tells us, "Compromise or suffer the consequences." But we're not going to do either one, because our God will help us possess the promises!

NUMBERS 23:19

19 "God is not a man, that He should lie, Nor a son of man, that He should repent. Has He said, and will He not do? Or has He spoken, and will He not make it good?"

What God has said will always come to pass in our lives if we'll trust Him. The Bible says that God cannot lie (Heb. 6:18). The Bible also says that Satan is a liar and the father of lies (John 8:44). What lies has the Enemy been whispering in your ear lately? His lies have no power over you if you will refute his lies with the irrefutable truth of God's Word!

When the Enemy whispers, "You're sick, and you can't get healed," you need to answer him with the Word of God: "By Jesus' stripes, I was healed!" (1 Peter 2:24). When Satan threatens, "You don't have any money, and you're never going to have any money," you need to answer him, "My God delights in my prosperity, and He will supply all my needs according to His riches in glory!" (Ps. 35:27; Phil. 4:19).

Whatever lie the devil tries to get you to believe and act on, know that his intention is always to *steal, kill,* and *destroy.* Find scriptures that promise what you need or desire. Get those promises deep in your heart by meditating on them and talking about them. Then continually speak those words out by faith and refuse to back down. God is leading you out of your difficulty by your faith in His Word, because He has already made a way for you to possess His promises!

Chapter 5

REMEMBERING GOD IN THE STORMS

There are times in the life of every believer, especially in the midst of tests and trials, when he or she will be tempted with the thought, *Is there really any blessing in living right before God and serving Him?* I didn't say every believer would *yield* to those thoughts and "throw in the towel" or walk away from God. But when we're encompassed with negative situations and circumstances, that's when the Enemy bombards us with thoughts of doubt, frustration, and confusion.

At times, we can feel overwhelmed and even feel as if the Enemy's forces are greater than the power of God. We look around and see many in the world prospering and acting as if they don't have a single care, while the righteous seem to go unrewarded. The ungodly blaspheme God continually, yet seem to prosper in everything they do. And we can be tempted to wonder, *What's wrong with this picture? Am I really on the right side?*

You might say, "Reverend Hagin, that seems a little far-fetched." But this was the prevailing attitude of the people of Judah when the prophet Nahum wrote the following words by the inspiration of the Holy Spirit.

NAHUM 1:7–9 (NIV)

7 The Lord is good, a refuge in times of trouble. He cares for those who trust in him,

8 but with an overwhelming flood he will make an end of Nineveh; he will pursue his foes into darkness.

9 Whatever they plot against the Lord he will bring to an end; trouble will not come a second time.

The people of Judah found themselves in the midst of very troubled times. Everything seemed to be going wrong for them. Sennacherib, king of Assyria, had brutally assaulted many of the cities of Judah. The people were forced to pay a tribute to the Assyrian king, who then tried to march on Jerusalem to overthrow it, but could not (see 2 Chron. 32:22). Judah and its capital city, Jerusalem, faced challenges on every side. On the other hand, Assyria and its capital city, Nineveh, appeared to prosper and flourish.

Have you ever faced a similar situation? You were serving God, yet everything seemed to be going wrong—while others around you were living ungodly lifestyles, yet seemed to be prospering at every turn.

I think we all have faced similar situations at one time or another. It's during times like these that we need to call for reinforcements from the Word of God! Our feelings that evil is prevailing are real, but they're just feelings—*not fact*—and they must take a back seat to the eternal truth of God's Holy Word!

Notice that Nahum said in verse 8: "...*With an overwhelming flood he will make an end of Nineveh; he will pursue his foes into darkness*" (NIV). The people of Judah were mired in their situation. They felt helpless, hopeless, and *stuck*! But here the prophet offers them hope. I can imagine he said something like this to God's people: "Although the enemy appears to be winning, the final score has not been posted. Don't lose heart. Keep your faith in God."

Naturally speaking, it seemed that God's people would never again be as affluent as they had been in the past. It looked as if they were helpless to extract themselves from the situation they were in. But then God came to them through the prophet and told them, "I will make a complete end of Nineveh." The Lord was telling them, "Your enemy may look as if they're prospering now. But the day will come when they will fall." And God did bring judgment on Nineveh. Some historians say the fall of that city in 612 B.C. occurred just a few years after Nahum's prophecy.

The Dangers of Dead Religion

In Scripture, Nineveh represents apostate religion—religion which has abandoned its former beliefs. And just as Nineveh was bent on destroying Jerusalem, apostate religion seeks to destroy true Christianity today.

Remember, the prophet Jonah had preached to this great city many years before. The people repented, and God's judgment was postponed. Yet years later, their ways did not reflect their repentance of the past.

The Apostle Paul identifies this type of religious crowd today by saying they "have a form of godliness, but deny its power" (2 Tim. 3:5). Then he said, *"From such people turn away!"* God warns us through Paul that there are people today who call themselves Christians, but who have renounced or forsaken certain fundamental beliefs. In other words, they may look right and they may talk right—but their lives do not reflect the true Gospel. They have a form or semblance of godliness, but by their actions, they deny the power of the glorious Gospel of Christ.

There is a vast difference between mere religion and true Christianity, or salvation through Christ. Religion proposes endless rules and regulations that one must follow to earn a spiritual standing, and it always brings bondage. True salvation was paid for by Christ and invites everyone to receive the free gift. To all who do, *freedom* is the result.

Now, don't misunderstand me. I'm not saying that receiving eternal salvation means that your conduct is irrelevant—that there's no "right and wrong," no code of conduct by which to live your life. I'm saying that the free gift of salvation through Christ ushers you into right standing with God. You're not bound by men's laws, but by God's eternal law of love and of grace through faith (see John 13:34; Eph. 2:8).

An Upward Look

In the midst of a great test or trial, you don't need someone telling you everything you may have done wrong or trying to give you 49 steps to victory. All you need to know is whose side you're on and that God is greater than any mistake or any challenge you'll ever face!

People often become so discouraged when they're facing a test or trial that they have a difficult time being positive. Sometimes a sense of shame causes them to look downward instead of upward. Whatever the reason, they need to know that a time of trouble is no time to run *away* from God. They must run *to* Him to find the answers they so desperately need.

Throughout the Word of God, no matter what the test or the circumstances surrounding the test, those who knew their God and understood His great love for them never entertained the idea of failure. They never even considered that they might not make it through their troubles. They were able to look beyond the present circumstances—beyond the "seen" realm—and focus on the unseen realm. They focused on the victory God had promised and prepared for them. They were buoyed up in faith and confidence in God, and they were able to remain optimistic despite their negative circumstances.

I am reminded of a story along this same line about a man who coached a Little League baseball team. During one of the games, the team began falling behind. In fact, they hadn't won very many games at all that season.

The coach entered the dugout to give his team a pep talk. He encouraged them, saying, "Now is not the time to have a pessimistic attitude."

One of the team members spoke up. "Coach, does 'pessimistic' mean that we think our team is going to lose?"

That's a pretty good definition of pessimism, isn't it! Pessimism is the attitude or mentality that you think you're going to lose. The voice of pessimism says, "Things are rough. We may not make it through this time." The voice of pessimism will hound and harass you to try to get you to give up before you ever get in the fight!

I like the song that Kenneth Copeland sings entitled "I Cannot Be Defeated." In fact, this is my theme song because some of the words in that song describe how I live my life. My personal motto for years has been, "I cannot be defeated and I will not quit." I've been through many tests and trials in my lifetime, but in each one, I always knew that God had prepared a way out for me. So I refused to quit and be defeated.

We should never give up on our faith in the midst of a test. God has prepared the way for each one of us to live in victory and overcome life's challenges. We can all have the attitude, *I cannot be defeated, and I will not quit!* If we will stick with God and His Word, He will cause us to triumph in every situation and circumstance (2 Cor. 2:14). In other words, we get to play until we win!

Proverbs 24:16 says, *"For a righteous man may fall seven times And rise again, But the wicked shall fall by calamity."* Notice this verse doesn't say, "A righteous man never falls." It says, in effect, that no matter how many times a righteous man falls down, he will keep rising up. In other words, he will not be defeated because he will not quit!

I believe that it's impossible to be defeated in life unless we simply refuse to trust God. In the midst of tests and troubles, it's important that we guard our hearts and our attitudes against lies from the Enemy that come against our minds to discourage and weaken us. We must be ready to refute the Enemy's lies with the irrefutable truth of God's Word!

Remembering Past Victories

When thoughts of fear and confusion bombard your mind, it's important to take those thoughts captive with the Word of God (2 Cor. 10:5). And as I mentioned previously, another thing you need to do is just be "still" before the Lord (Ps. 46:10).

Something that always helps me when I'm tempted to be discouraged is to remember the great things God has already done for me. He has seen me through so many tough times in the past. Remembering the ways He has already blessed me helps me focus on the future with hope instead of despair.

Is there anything you can thank God for that He has already done for you? Has He saved you from a sinner's hell? Has He provided for your needs? Do you have food to eat? Do you have a roof over your head?

Too many times when things aren't going the way we'd like them to go, we fret or complain as if God has forsaken us! That's what happened to the children of Israel in the wilderness after they supernaturally escaped the bondage of Egypt.

Through many spectacular, miraculous acts of God, the Israelites were delivered from Pharaoh and their Egyptian taskmasters. Yet not long after their deliverance, they began to get hungry. So they turned on Moses, saying, "... *'Oh, that we had died by the hand of the Lord in the land of Egypt, when we sat by the pots of meat and when we ate bread to the full! For you have brought us out into this wilderness to kill this whole assembly with hunger'"* (Exod. 16:3).

In fact, every time the Israelites encountered any kind of difficulty, they murmured and complained against Moses and against the Lord. They weren't remembering past victories. In fact, it often appears that they had completely forgotten them—the plagues of Egypt, the parting of the Red Sea, the cloud by day and the fire by night, and the bread from Heaven that God rained down from the sky each day to sustain them!

Why is knowing this important for us today? Paul said, *"All these things happened to them as EXAMPLES, and they were written for our ADMONITION . . ."* (1 Cor. 10:11). The Lord wants us to learn from the successes of the men and women of the Bible. But He also wants us to learn from their failures and mistakes!

One mistake the Israelites made was failing to remember properly the great things the Lord had done for them. We should constantly remind ourselves of every victory God has granted us. Yet how quickly many of us forget!

Remember That God Is Strong and Mighty

When the storms of life are brewing on the horizon, and the skies appear dark and ominous, we must hold steady so we can stay the course in the midst of the storm. And we must not give way to fear and other negative emotions.

In Judah's case, the people had become discouraged. They were burdened because of the Assyrians' yoke that was upon them.

God sent His prophet to encourage them, and the first thing Nahum told them was how mighty God is!

NAHUM 1:3-6

3 The Lord is slow to anger and great in power, And will not at all acquit the wicked. The Lord has His way In the whirlwind and in the storm, And the clouds are the dust of His feet.

4 He rebukes the sea and makes it dry, And dries up all the rivers. Bashan and Carmel wither, And the flower of Lebanon wilts.

5 The mountains quake before Him, The hills melt, And the earth heaves at His presence, Yes, the world and all who dwell in it.

6 Who can stand before His indignation? And who can endure the fierceness of His anger? His fury is poured out like fire, And the rocks are thrown down by Him.

When the Enemy is closing in and threatening you to try to make you weak with fear, remember that the Lord your God is strong and mighty—and that He is on your side!

Most people would agree that God is powerful and strong. But many who acknowledge God's strength and power see God as distant and removed from their personal lives. In other words, they see Him as strong, but they don't necessarily see His strength as benefiting *them*. But Proverbs 18:10 says, *"The name of the Lord is a STRONG tower; The righteous run to it and are safe."* The righteous can run to God and find protection and safety. They can have a personal knowledge of a strong and mighty God in their lives.

God Wants You to Be Strong in the Storm!

Not only does God want to show Himself strong on your behalf, but He wants *you* to be strong in the midst of a test or trial. Ephesians 6:10 says, *". . . be strong in the Lord and in the power of His might."*

"How do I do that?" you might ask.

Isaiah 40:31 says, *"Those who wait on the Lord shall renew their strength; They shall mount up with wings like eagles, They shall run and not be weary, They shall walk and not faint."*

What does it mean to "mount up with wings like eagles"? The eagle is a majestic bird with the innate ability to soar at tremendous heights of up to 10,000 feet. Similarly, we as Christians have the ability to "soar" high above the tests and trials of life.

The wings of the eagle are long and wide, and tapered at the end with smaller feathers that separate like fingers. Updrafts or thermals—warm pockets of air that rise—allow the eagle to soar at great heights. The only time the eagle has to flap its wings is to fly above another thermal. There it glides effortlessly, conserving energy and maintaining tremendous stamina. Most eagles can fly up to 150 miles per day, and during migration, they can fly almost twice that distance.

What's especially amazing about the eagle is what it does when a storm comes. The eagle doesn't hide from a storm, no matter how fierce the winds. At the first signs of a storm, the eagle rises high above the disturbance. The eagle doesn't *suffer through* the storm or even *weather* the storm. It simply rises high above it on the very winds that brought the storm in the first place.

We can learn a valuable lesson from the eagle. Storms come to us all, but if we wait upon the Lord, we can rise above them. We don't have to give place to discouragement, hopelessness, despair, or defeat.

Actually, it's not the storms of life that defeat us. It's how we respond to the storms that determine our outcome. We all need to be more like the eagle, worshipping and waiting on the Lord and rising high above the storms of life, where we can see our challenges from Heaven's point of view—from the viewpoint of victory.

What are the effects of waiting upon the Lord and mounting up "with wings like eagles"? The result will be strength and steadfast endurance—the kind of strength and stamina that defeats the storms of life and wins great victories.

'Hitting the Wall'

The rest of Isaiah 40:31 says, ". . . *They shall run and not be weary, they shall walk and not faint.*" Have you ever run a distance race or watched someone else run a race? Runners will tell you that in running long distances, there comes a point in the race called the "runner's wall" at which you must decide whether to quit or to get your second wind. If you forge through that "wall," you pick up a fresh, new burst of energy, and you feel almost as if you could run forever!

As we're running our spiritual race, tests and trials and feelings of discouragement can make us tired. We can feel as if we want to quit. But waiting upon the Lord, spending time in His

Presence just worshipping Him, will give us our "second wind." That enables us to stay in the race and win the victories that God intends for us to win. As we wait upon the Lord, we receive the strength to "run and not be weary" and to "walk and not faint."

In chapter 3 of this book, we looked at a group of Israelites who doubted God because they believed the circumstances—the giants in the land of Canaan—more than they believed God's Word. God said that He had given them the land, but they fainted with fear at the sight of the giants. They declared, "We are as grasshoppers in their sight" (Num. 13:33).

These doubters had forgotten all the miracles God performed on their behalf to get them right to the edge of the Promised Land. They quit just short of receiving the promise because they failed to remember God in troubled times. They failed to remember that He is strong and mighty.

However, two men—Joshua and Caleb—remembered the Lord's strength, declaring, "We are well able to overcome" (Num. 13:30). And after God allowed an entire unbelieving generation of Israelites to die in the wilderness, those two men marched into the land with a new generation and possessed the promises of God!

Remember That God Is Good

After Nahum hailed the mighty acts and the power of God, the prophet encouraged the people concerning God's goodness.

NAHUM 1:7 (NIV)

7 The Lord is good, a refuge in times of trouble. He cares for those who trust in him . . .

Notice Nahum didn't just tell the people that God is good. He told them what embracing God's goodness would mean to them. In essence, Nahum said, "God will be your refuge, your stronghold, in these troubled times. He will care for you, keeping watch over you and protecting you." In other words, Nahum encouraged the people of Judah not only that God is good, but that He would do something to benefit them.

If you knew of a generous multimillionaire who gave money to several good causes, you might say about him, "He's a good person." But if you were in dire need and that same multimillionaire said, "I want to help *you*," your attitude would take on an entirely new perspective. Not only would you say, "That man is good," but you would also say, "That man is good to *me*"!

You see, the goodness of God is only significant to people if they believe God will be good to *them*. But God's very act of sending Jesus to redeem mankind shows His willingness to be good to all. When the angel appeared to the shepherds in the field and announced the Savior's birth, a heavenly host appeared with him, exclaiming, "'Glory to God in the highest, And on earth peace, GOODWILL toward men!'" (Luke 2:14).

The goodness of God is tied to the provision of God. God wants to be your Provider, but it's your belief in His goodness that releases His provision. What do you need today? If you will look to God and "remember" Him in the midst of your trouble—that He is strong and mighty and that He is good—He will see you through whatever challenges you're facing.

Remember That God Is Faithful

What is the one quality that comes to mind when you think of someone who's faithful? When someone is faithful, that person is trustworthy, right? In other words, that person can be depended on. If he makes a promise, you can be certain that he will make good on his word, because he's *faithful*.

What about God? Is He faithful and trustworthy? Can He be depended on in times of trouble? Without a doubt, yes, He can! He can bring to pass every promise and make an utter end of your problem, causing that burden or challenge to become a thing of the past.

That's precisely what Nahum said to Judah concerning their oppression by the Assyrians. He declared to them the *strength* of God, the *goodness* of God, and the *faithfulness* of God. Look at what the Lord promised His people concerning the Assyrian city of Nineveh.

NAHUM 1:9 (NIV)

9 Whatever they plot against the Lord he will bring to an end; trouble will not come a second time.

NAHUM 1:9 (NASB)

9 Whatever you devise against the Lord, He will make a complete end of it. Distress will not rise up twice.

God in His faithfulness promised an end to Judah's troubles. Nahum was trying to encourage the people to take hold of the promise of God and remember God's faithfulness.

Years before this time, a generation of Israelites had failed to lay hold of God's promise to possess the land where the people of Judah were now living. After all the miracles God had performed in delivering His people from Egypt and guiding them in the wilderness on their way to their Promised Land, they fell short of receiving the promise because they failed to trust the Lord. They failed to remember the faithfulness of God.

Notice what the psalmist says concerning the importance of trusting God.

PSALM 37:39-40

39 But the salvation of the righteous is from the Lord: He is their strength in the time of trouble.

40 And the Lord shall help them and deliver them; He shall deliver them from the wicked, And save them, BECAUSE THEY TRUST IN HIM.

Receiving victory and deliverance really is a matter of trust. Who—or what—are you trusting in to help you in troubled times? Are you trusting in a person to help you? Or are you trusting in the bank, the economy, or the government to put you over? Perhaps you're trusting in *yourself* to obtain the victory you desire.

Oftentimes in the midst of difficulty, we stop following God because we're trying to figure out the answer to our problem on our own. But if we could have done something about our problem or difficulty, we would have already done it! When we try to fix our own problems apart from God, we usually gain a whole new set of problems. We may have started out believing and trusting

God, but now we're holding on tightly to the situation. That means we're tying God's hands even though He desires to help us.

When we find ourselves tempted to take back a problem that we've already turned over to the Lord, that's when we need to stop and put ourselves in remembrance of the faithfulness of God. First Peter 5:7 says, ". . . *casting all your care upon Him, for He cares for you.*" When we cast our cares on the Lord, we must leave them in His care and keeping. Only then can we truly believe that God will see us safely through our test or trial.

When you give your troubles to God, you can go to bed at night and sleep peacefully. If you're tossing and turning and staying up all night because of some problem or difficulty, you probably haven't "cast the care" of that problem on the Lord. You've still got a firm grip on it. Rather, the problem has a firm grip on you!

The worst thing you could do in troubled times is to forget the faithfulness of God. You need to keep your feet planted firmly on the integrity of His Word and refuse to budge. God has said, "I will be with you in trouble" (Ps. 91:15). He also said, "I will never leave you, nor forsake you" (Heb. 13:5).

I tell you, I would rather know that God is with me than to hear any economic or political expert attempt to comfort me or give me hope. I know that when God says, "I will help you and provide for you," I can depend on His faithfulness no matter what the economic or political tides. He is the same "yesterday, today, and forever" (Heb. 13:8). He can be trusted to keep His Word in times of plenty and in times of scarcity and lack. He is the Lord Who changes not (Mal. 3:6)!

When God promises something from His Word, you can count on His faithfulness to make it happen. No matter how fierce the storm or how big the giant, you will "cross over to the other side" victoriously if you will remember God in troubled times. In fact, the only way your promise *won't* come to pass is if you give up and quit believing, if you turn your back on God.

The mistakes the children of Israel made don't have to be our mistakes today. In troubled times, we must remember God and His Word. We must never forget His strength, power, and ability to help us, and we must never forget His goodness—His willingness to help us. Lastly, we must never forget God's faithfulness, because every word He promises, He is able to perform!

Chapter 6

FACING THE GIANTS

There are many powerful lessons we can learn from the battles the Israelites had to fight in order to possess the Promised Land. For example, we know that we must fight spiritual battles in order to possess the blessings that God has promised us today.

The Apostle Paul wrote the following words to Timothy, his son in the faith: *"Fight the good fight of faith, lay hold on eternal life, to which you were also called and have confessed the good confession in the presence of many witnesses"* (1 Tim. 6:12). This verse tells us, among other things, that there is a "fight" to faith.

In his teachings on the subject of faith, my father used to say, "The blessings of God don't fall on us like ripe cherries off a tree." He was implying that appropriating the promises of God takes some effort on our part. Yet we know that many Christians who want the blessings of God also want someone else to obtain those blessings for them.

The Bible says that the just shall live by faith (Hab. 2:4; Rom. 1:17; Gal. 3:11; Heb. 10:38). It also says, *". . . faith comes by hearing, and hearing by the word of God"* (Rom. 10:17). But many Christians don't want to read, study, or meditate on the Word of God for themselves. They don't want to submit to the "hearing of faith." They want someone else to use his or her faith on their behalf.

When believers are spiritual babies, it's easy to "carry" them with our faith. But every believer is called to grow and to stand on his own two feet, spiritually speaking. God wants him to enjoy his own individual walk with the Lord and receive the blessings of God for himself.

Certainly, it's not wrong for a believer to ask someone else to pray for him. But if that believer never learns to pray for himself, he will never know the joy of trusting God personally. Inevitably, there will come a time when he is confronted with a "giant"— some challenge or test—but if he hasn't learned to "fight the good fight of faith" on his own, he will be unprepared for the battle that lies before him.

Obviously, the giants we face today aren't physical giants like the ones who challenged the Israelites. Nevertheless, there are lessons we can learn from such encounters that will help us deal victoriously with the obstacles and challenges that loom like giants before us today.

I want to look at one particular giant that threatened an entire nation, yet only one young man was courageous enough to stand against him. I'm talking about the battle between the giant Goliath and God's covenant man David.

Please read carefully the following passage from First Samuel chapter 17.

1 SAMUEL 17:2–11

2 And Saul and the men of Israel were gathered together, and they encamped in the Valley of Elah, and drew up in battle array against the Philistines.

3 The Philistines stood on a mountain on one side, and Israel stood on a mountain on the other side, with a valley between them.

4 And a champion went out from the camp of the Philistines, named Goliath, from Gath, WHOSE HEIGHT WAS SIX CUBITS AND A SPAN.

5 He had a bronze helmet on his head, and he was armed with a coat of mail, and the weight of the coat was five thousand shekels of bronze.

6 And he had bronze armor on his legs and a bronze javelin between his shoulders.

7 Now the staff of his spear was like a weaver's beam, and his iron spearhead weighed six hundred shekels; and a shield-bearer went before him.

8 Then he stood and cried out to the armies of Israel, and said to them, "Why have you come out to line up for battle? Am I not a Philistine, and you the servants of Saul? Choose a man for yourselves, and let him come down to me.

9 "If he is able to fight with me and kill me, then we will be your servants. But if I prevail against him and kill him, then you shall be our servants and serve us."

10 And the Philistine said, "I defy the armies of Israel this day; give me a man, that we may fight together."

11 WHEN SAUL AND ALL ISRAEL [the Israelite army] HEARD THESE WORDS of the Philistine, THEY WERE DISMAYED AND GREATLY AFRAID.

When giants confront us in the form of tests and trials, the Enemy taunts us to try to intimidate us, just as Goliath intimidated the armies of Israel. Satan exaggerates his own power and abilities and raises doubts in our mind concerning God's willingness or ability to help us. His goal is to cause us to be "dismayed and greatly afraid."

Facing the Giants With Faith or Fear?

Now, Goliath was no small threat to the Israelites. He was a real giant—more than nine feet tall! Similarly, we can face real tests and trials in life that are "larger than life" and impossible to overcome in our own strength or might. Nevertheless, even in times of extraordinary crises, victory is not far away when we're walking with God. He will defend us! But, like David, we must face the giant with confidence, instead of running from it in fear.

What about Goliath's armor? Verse 5 says Goliath's helmet was made of bronze, and the weight of his "coat of mail" was well over 100 pounds. Verse 7 says that just the iron spearhead on the giant's spear weighed about 15 pounds. Goliath's entire suit of armor, including his helmet and spear, could have weighed in the vicinity of 200 pounds!

If you know anything about track-and-field, you know that in high school, a shot put weighs eight or nine pounds. In college, the standard shot put weight is 16 pounds. When I ran track in high school, I was a sprinter, and I was good at what I did. But I was not built or conditioned to throw the shot put—I weighed only 145 pounds soaking wet! The guy who threw the shot put for our team weighed about 250 pounds, and he threw it almost like you'd throw a baseball! Now, I could pick up the shot put easily enough. But to throw it the distances he threw it would have been impossible for me from a natural standpoint.

Can you imagine the strength needed for Goliath to throw his spear with any degree of force and accuracy? If the top of his spear alone weighed more than 15 pounds, I guarantee you, this guy was a heavyweight!

Not only was Goliath an experienced fighter of magnificent strength, but he was also very arrogant. He said, *". . . 'I defy the armies of Israel this day' . . ."* (v. 10). And in defying the armies of Israel, he was also defying Israel's God.

The Israelites knew from experience the saving, delivering power of God. Yet because one ungodly man stood against them, roaring about what he was going to do to them, they became paralyzed with fear. We know this is true because Goliath's challenge went unanswered for 40 days: *"And the Philistine drew near and presented himself forty days, morning and evening"* (v. 16).

While Goliath swaggered and strutted in arrogance and pride, the Israelites were completely incapacitated by fear. The armies of Israel and the armies of Philistia were arrayed against one another. But not one bow had been drawn or one spear thrown. Yet the Israelites, by all appearances, were deflated and defeated. It wasn't Goliath who had defeated them; it was their own fear!

It's easy to read these verses in the Bible and see the mistake the Israelites made in allowing themselves to be intimidated by Goliath. But how many times have we "run scared" at the first sign of a challenge? The devil tried to tell us something, such as, "You have an incurable disease, and you're going to die," or, "You're going to go broke and lose your home," and we felt completely helpless and hopeless against Satan's threats.

Often, we're so overcome by the lies and taunts of the Enemy that we're defeated before we even try to fight. The devil knows that if he can get us to yield to fear and to remain in fear, he will win the battle. Why? Because fear confuses our thinking and causes us to believe, speak, or act, contrary to the truth of God's Word.

1 SAMUEL 17:17–18

17 Then Jesse said to his son David, "Take now for your brothers an ephah of this dried grain and these ten loaves, and run to your brothers at the camp.

18 And carry these ten cheeses to the captain of their thousand, and see how your brothers fare, and bring back news of them."

David had seven brothers, and the three oldest brothers were serving in Saul's armies. David's father had sent David to the camp with supplies. As David arrived, he heard Goliath's taunts and threats.

1 SAMUEL 17:25–26

25 So the men of Israel said, "Have you seen this man who has come up? Surely he has come up to defy Israel; and it shall be that the man who kills him the king will enrich with great riches, will give him his daughter, and give his father's house exemption from taxes in Israel."

26 Then David spoke to the men who stood by him, saying, "What shall be done for the man who kills this Philistine and takes away the reproach from Israel? For who is this uncircumcised Philistine, that he should defy the armies of the living God?"

I want you to notice that David's reaction was completely oppo-site that of Israel's fighting army. Upon hearing the enemy's threats, David maintained his composure and even became indignant. David said, "... *who IS this uncircumcised Philistine, that he should defy the armies of the living God?*" In our language today, we might paraphrase David as saying, "Who does this guy think he is!"

Stirred to Action

David's attitude was one of righteous indignation that this Philistine would so blatantly blaspheme the Living God. In the same way, we should become righteously indignant when the devil proposes that we accept defeat. When we see an injustice in our lives or in the lives of others, we should be stirred to action, break-ing out of our cloak of apathy or fear.

For example, when you *know that you know* what the Bible says about healing, and you understand that it is God's will that you be healed and live life whole, you should be indignant at the first symptom of sickness or disease that tries to come against your body. You should instantly answer it with the Word of God, saying, "How *dare* you defy the Word of the Living God, which says, 'By His stripes, we are healed'" (1 Pet. 2:24)!

God is God—He was, is, and always will be Almighty God! As believers today, we should be quick to take a stand against the oppression of the world that tries to creep into the Church and into our lives personally. Whether it's sin, sickness, disease, or poverty, we should resist it with the weapon of the Word of God on our lips, refusing to be defeated or give up and quit.

Where Is Your Confidence in Troubled Times?

Upon hearing the threats of the enemy Goliath, look at David's response and call to action.

1 SAMUEL 17:32

32 Then David said to Saul, "Let no man's heart fail because of him; your servant will go and fight with this Philistine."

Goliath was arrogant, but David possessed a greater inner strength and determination than the giant because David was supremely confident—not in himself, but in his God!

Arrogance "mouths off," as we saw in the actions of Goliath. Nothing he said was based on truth. Goliath was full of pride because of his great size and strength and because of his past accomplishments. But David's statements were based on the truth of the Living God, in Whom David had placed his complete confidence and trust. In other words, David was depending on God to back up his words. Goliath had only himself and his own abilities to depend on. Truly, this was not an even match!

More than any of Israel's fighting men, David understood his position with God. David understood his covenant, and he had an experience with God. In other words, his knowledge of God didn't come just from hearing the Law taught or from hearing about someone else's experience. David had an experience of his own.

1 SAMUEL 17:33-37

33 And Saul said to David, "You are not able to go against this Philistine to fight with him; for you are a youth, and he a man of war from his youth."

34 But David said to Saul, "Your servant used to keep his father's sheep, and when a lion or a bear came and took a lamb out of the flock,

35 I went out after it and struck it, and delivered the lamb from its mouth; and when it arose against me, I caught it by its beard, and struck and killed it.

36 Your servant has killed both lion and bear; and this uncircumcised Philistine will be like one of them, seeing he has defied the armies of the living God."

37 Moreover David said, "The Lord, who delivered me from the paw of the lion and from the paw of the bear, He will deliver me from the hand of this Philistine." And Saul said to David, "Go, and the Lord be with you!"

David didn't just decide to walk with God when confronted with a giant in the heat of battle. David had walked with God even while he was out shepherding his father's sheep. David rehearsed before Saul his experiences of defending his father's sheep against both "lion and bear" (vv. 34–36). This young shepherd boy was prepared for the battle that lay before him because of his experiences with God in the past.

Courage comes from quiet faith and strong belief in God and His righteousness, even in the hard times. David no doubt had grown up hearing about the mighty acts of God. But when his father's sheep were confronted with danger, David put his faith into action and experienced victories in the midst of challenges. David didn't turn and run at the first sign of a lion or a bear. Instead, he took up his position because he knew his God, and he knew that God would help him. That's why David could so confidently say to Saul, ". . . *The Lord, who delivered me from the paw of the lion and from the paw of the bear, He will deliver me from the hand of this Philistine'"* (v. 37).

Your 'Tested' Weapons of Victory

When King Saul finally agreed to allow David to square off against the giant, he outfitted David with his own weaponry. He placed on David's head a bronze helmet and clothed him with a coat of armor. David fastened his sword to Saul's armor and tried to walk. Suddenly, he stopped and said to the king, *". . . 'I cannot walk with these, for I have not tested them' . . ."* (v. 39). The *King James Version* says, *". . . I cannot go with these; for I have not proved them."* Then David removed the king's armor. David wouldn't step out using what worked for someone else; he wanted to step out using what had worked for him.

During my basic training in the Army, I witnessed a similar encounter I will never forget. There was a young man in our platoon who had grown up in the hills of Kentucky. We happened to be in the last training regiment that ever trained with the old M-1 rifle. Our sergeant commander was explaining how to use the sights on our rifles when he noticed that this fellow from Kentucky wasn't paying very close attention. The sergeant reprimanded the young man. The enlistee lost his cool and retorted, "I can shoot the eye out of a squirrel with a .22 caliber from 50 yards! *Can you?*"

Just at the time the young man said this, our lieutenant happened to be walking by. The lieutenant said to both of them, "I tell you what. Let's just have a little shooting contest!"

We were out on the firing range, so they set up the targets, and the lieutenant said, "Each of you can zero in on your target any way you want to."

The sergeant shot first. The clip in our guns held eight .30-caliber shells. He wrapped the sling around his arm and assumed the prone position just like he was supposed to. The sergeant got off his eight shots, landing four inside the range of the bull's eye and four around the outside of the target.

Then it was the young soldier's turn. He licked his finger two or three times and held it up each time, as if checking for wind direction. Then he assumed his position and emptied all eight of his shots in the dead center of that bull's eye!

During the rest of our training, no one ever instructed that soldier again on how to fire a weapon. And when graduation time came, he was awarded several honors for marksmanship, receiving the highest marks—not just of anyone in our platoon, but in the entire battalion! This young man even received a special citation from the battalion commander.

The soldier told several of us later, "I never even use a sight, because the sight on my rifle at home broke, and I never replaced it. I shot my first squirrel at the age of four, and I've been hunting with my father ever since. In fact, growing up, we never bought meat from a grocery store. We went out into the woods and killed our meat!"

Like David, this soldier used his own past encounters to win present victories. He didn't rely on the experiences of others, and neither should we. It's great to be inspired by the experiences of others. But we need to develop our own walk with God and have experiences of our own.

Remember, John 8:32 says, " *'You shall know the truth, and the truth shall make you free.'* " In other words, it's not just the truth that makes you free; it's the truth that you *know* that makes you free. We could take that a step further and say that it's the truth that you know personally that makes you truly free. The truth that someone else knows may help or inspire you. But if you don't study that truth and learn it for yourself, you will find yourself at a disadvantage in life.

You're only going to be able to defeat the giants in your life with what *you* know about God and His Word. That's why it's important to read, study, and meditate on the Word until it becomes a part of you—in your spirit and not just in your head.

Make Your Boast in the Lord, Not in Yourself

Let's continue reading in First Samuel chapter 17.

1 SAMUEL 17:42-44

42 And when the Philistine looked about and saw David, he disdained him; for he was only a youth, ruddy and good-looking.

43 So the Philistine said to David, "Am I a dog, that you come to me with sticks?" And the Philistine cursed David by his gods.

44 And the Philistine said to David, "Come to me, and I will give your flesh to the birds of the air and the beasts of the field!"

Notice the pride and arrogance of the Philistine giant. When he saw David's demeanor and determined that he was but a youth and not a man of war, he was insulted. He became very angry and cursed David.

How did David respond? Did he respond in kind, returning railing for railing or making idle threats against the giant? No, David confidently made his boast in what *God* was going to do!

1 SAMUEL 17:45–47

45 Then David said to the Philistine, "You come to me with a sword, with a spear, and with a javelin. But I come to you IN THE NAME OF THE LORD OF HOSTS, THE GOD OF THE ARMIES OF ISRAEL, whom you have defied.

46 This day THE LORD WILL DELIVER YOU INTO MY HAND, and I will strike you and take your head from you. And this day I will give the carcasses of the camp of the Philistines to the birds of the air and the wild beasts of the earth, THAT ALL THE EARTH MAY KNOW THAT THERE IS A GOD IN ISRAEL.

47 Then all this assembly shall know that THE LORD DOES NOT SAVE WITH SWORD AND SPEAR; for THE BATTLE IS THE LORD'S, and HE WILL GIVE YOU INTO OUR HANDS."

David was talking covenant talk! He never made a single assertion that took attention away from God and focused just on himself.

I have heard believers talk about how they were going to "storm hell's gates" and defeat the Enemy in spiritual battle. I understood what they were saying. I don't think they really believed they were going to stand against some giant in their life in just their own strength and might. But we need to be careful to give all the glory to God when we're fighting the good fight of faith.

The Bible says that pride goes before a fall (Prov. 16:18). If we're not careful, we can begin to think that we're "something special" when it comes to doing spiritual battle. We can forget that Jesus is the One Who stormed hell's gates and defeated the Enemy once and for all through His death, burial, and resurrection. All that remains for us to do is to stand our ground in faith, based on Christ's finished work. And we must remember that as we do, our present battles are the Lord's. If we will stand our ground on His infallible Word, He will fight for us!

1 SAMUEL 17:48

48 So it was, when the Philistine arose and came and drew near to meet David, that David hurried and ran toward the army to meet the Philistine.

Notice that when the Philistine began moving toward David, David ran toward him. David wasn't charging the giant in his own might. He was going in the strength of the Lord, depending on God to fight for him.

The Word of God in Battle:
How to Stay on the Offensive

Too many times when the Enemy comes toward us, we either stand there and wait for the attack, or we run away in terror! We offer no resistance. And then we wonder why God doesn't do something about the devil for us! But James 4:7 says, "*Submit to God. Resist the devil and he will flee from you.*" The understood subject in that verse is "you." In other words, God is saying, "*You resist the devil, and he will flee from you.*" We've let the devil put us on the run when we should have been resisting him and putting *him* on the run!

Boxing coaches often tell their boxers, "You must get off the first punch." In other words, we shouldn't wait for our spiritual opponents to strike first. When we have God's Word in our hearts, we need to get on the offensive with that Word on our lips!

In the same sense, that's what David did, and we know what happened as a result.

1 SAMUEL 17:49–52

49 Then David put his hand in his bag and took out a stone; and he slung it and struck the Philistine in his forehead, so that the stone sank into his forehead, and he fell on his face to the earth.

50 So David prevailed over the Philistine with a sling and a stone, and struck the Philistine and killed him. But there was no sword in the hand of David.

51 Therefore David ran and stood over the Philistine, took his sword and drew it out of its sheath and killed him, and cut off his head with it. And when the Philistines saw that their champion was dead, they fled.

52 Now the men of Israel and Judah arose and shouted, and pursued the Philistines as far as the entrance of the valley and to the gates of Ekron. And the wounded of the Philistines fell along the road to Shaaraim, even as far as Gath and Ekron.

When you're walking with God, the "giants" have no real authority in your life. But as long as you're on this earth, they are going to attempt to "face off" with you and challenge your faith and confidence in God. As I said previously, the Enemy will challenge you to see if you really believe what you *say* you believe.

Is your faith in God and His Word mere head knowledge or lip service? Or will you hasten to the battle when the Enemy tries to defeat you or take you captive in some way? With God's Word in your heart and on your lips, you can face the giants in life and defeat every spiritual foe, bringing glory to the One Who will fight for you and win!

Chapter 7

HOW TO BE A GIANT KILLER

Previously, we saw that David stood up to and defeated a giant who had threatened the existence of Israel. We also looked in some detail at the Israelites, who were confronted by giants at the edge of the Promised Land. We saw that the first generation of Israelites weren't giant killers at all. In fact, they refused to even face the giants that were living in the land God had promised them!

What did that generation of believers lack when they proclaimed, "We're not able to overcome"? They lacked faith in God's Word when He said that He had already given them the land. They had heard the promise, yet they refused to budge. And they were defeated in life as a result. They fell short of living the life God intended for them.

Now let's observe another generation that traversed the wilderness under Moses' leadership—the sons and daughters of those who refused to believe God and enter the land of their inheritance.

After Moses died and Joshua became the leader of the people of Israel, this generation of believers, including Caleb, finally possessed the blessing and received their promised inheritance. Some 45 years after Moses sent the 12 spies into Canaan, this new generation said to Joshua, ". . . *'All that you command us we will do, and wherever you send us we will go'*" (Josh. 1:16). In other words, they said, "Let's do it!"

Remember, after Moses had sent the 12 spies into the land of Canaan, only two of the 12—Joshua and Caleb—remained steadfast in their faith after they saw the giants that were living in the land. The other ten spies were moved by the obstacles and challenges they knew they would have to face in order to obtain what God had promised.

A Man With 'Giant' Faith in God

Now I want to focus on Caleb's attitude toward the giants that he, along with all the others, had witnessed in the Promised Land.

NUMBERS 13:30

30 Then Caleb quieted the people before Moses, and said, "LET US GO UP AT ONCE AND TAKE POSSESSION, FOR WE ARE WELL ABLE TO OVERCOME IT."

I like Caleb's spirit. He had the spirit of a giant killer! After he gave his faith-filled report, the ten unbelieving spies tried to nullify Caleb's faith. I can just imagine Caleb reasoning with the others: "Look, people, God has already given us the land. How hard can this be if He has already said the land belongs to us? With the Lord's help, we can do this!"

The ten spies were defeatists. In essence, they said, "Sure, the land is rich and fertile, but no way are we going in there—we'll be devoured by giants!" (Num. 13:31–32).

There were numerous giants in southern Canaan, the territory that led to the mountainous region of the Promised Land. Yet many years later, after the Israelites finally began to possess the land, Caleb still had his eye on one of those mountains. Although the mountain was inhabited by giants, Caleb declared with unflinching faith, "I want that one!" (see Josh. 14:12).

Seeing the Giant Killer in You!

What about you? Do you see yourself as a giant killer or as giant *bait*? Caleb saw himself as a giant killer. He had confidence in God that whatever stood in the way of possessing what God had promised would have to move or be moved!

On the other hand, the ten unbelieving spies saw themselves as giant bait—grasshoppers in the sight of Canaan's giants.

NUMBERS 13:31-33

31 The men who had gone up with him said, "We are not able to go up against the people, for they are stronger than we."

32 And they gave the children of Israel a bad report of the land which they had spied out, saying, "The land through which we have gone as spies is a land that devours its inhabitants, and all the people whom we saw in it are men of great stature.

33 There we saw the giants (the descendants of Anak came from the giants); and WE WERE LIKE GRASSHOPPERS IN OUR OWN SIGHT, AND SO WE WERE IN THEIR SIGHT."

Proverbs 23:7 tells us that the thoughts of a person's heart define the person: *"For as he thinks in his heart, so is he."* The ten spies were no exception. They were defined by the thoughts of their hearts. They had a "grasshopper" attitude or mentality, and that's what they were in reality—"grasshoppers" incapable of withstanding life's challenges and possessing the promises of God by faith.

If we are going to receive and enjoy the blessings of God as He intends, we must have a giant-killer mentality. When we see a promise in God's Word, like Caleb, we must have the attitude, *Give me this mountain!* We must be willing to face the giants of sickness, lack, doubt, fear, and all spiritual opposition that attempts to hinder us from receiving from God. Our success depends on how we see ourselves—as giant killers or giant *bait!*

Identify the 'Giant' Within You!

The greatest key to the success of those who have possessed their promises is their great confidence in a great God. Similarly, we're going to have to look to God, too, if we're to possess our promised blessings.

So the first thing you must do to become a giant killer is to identify the "Giant" within you.

1 JOHN 4:4 (KJV)

4 Ye are of God, little children, and have overcome them: because GREATER IS HE THAT IS IN YOU, THAN HE THAT IS IN THE WORLD.

We need to live conscious and aware of the Holy Spirit within us. If we've been born again, the Holy Spirit lives within our re-created spirit—and He is the greatest power in this universe!

Many Christians don't understand the vital role of the Holy Spirit in their lives. But He was sent to help us overcome the giants standing between us and our blessings. Jesus said in John 16:7, *"Nevertheless I tell you the truth. It is to your advantage that I go away; for if I do not go away, the Helper will not come to you; but if I depart, I will send Him to you."*

I encourage you to look up the many scriptures that talk about the role of the Holy Spirit in the life of the believer today. The Holy Spirit will be a Comforter, Counselor, Advocate, Intercessor, and Strengthener to you. He is greater than the devil and all of his cohorts. He is the Spirit that raised Jesus Christ from the dead and defeated Satan in hell's awful combat. And He lives in *you*!

The Greater One—the Holy Spirit—is the "Giant" that lives inside each of us as believers. Because this is true, when you stand against the giants of life, you have more wisdom than the problem that needs to be solved, more light than the darkness that tries to obscure, more strength than the cares that can weigh you down, and more stamina than the test or trial at hand. No matter what giant is attacking you, your "Giant" is *greater*!

We must learn to depend upon the Greater One Who lives within. Thank God for our God-given ability to think and reason. Thank God for the things we know in the natural. But there are times in our lives when nothing but the wisdom of God and the counsel of the Holy Spirit will do. He stands ready and willing to help us. We must continually be conscious and aware of His Presence.

The power of the Holy Spirit is not limited to being in one place at one time, and His wisdom is not limited to the wisdom of man. God is omnipotent, omnipresent, and omniscient. There is no giant anywhere that can defeat you when you realize the infinite power, the Presence, and the knowledge of the Greater One Who resides in you!

Identify the Giant You're Facing

One of the most important things you must do to become a giant killer is to identify the giant, or challenge, you're facing. My father used to always say, "Son, if you're going to stand your ground in faith, you have to know what you're standing against." It is a timeless truth that before you can fix a problem, you have to know what the problem is.

Addiction is a "giant" in this country that has ruined many a life and robbed many of the joy of becoming all God created them to be. There are certain groups that deal very successfully with addictions, such as drug addiction, alcohol addition, sex addiction, gambling addiction, and so forth. And every one of those groups will tell you that the very first step to recovery is admitting that you have a problem. Once a person does that and is sincere, the battle may be long, but it's already half over. Why? The giant that has held him or her back for so long has been exposed!

We must identify the giant that is confronting us and trying to hinder us from possessing our promise from God. But some are afraid to identify their enemy. They operate on the premise, "Ignorance is bliss. What I don't know won't hurt me." But sometimes what you don't know, or what you refuse to acknowledge, can kill you!

What's in a Name?

Although it *is* important that we identify the giant that we're facing, we don't need to get caught up in names. For example, some people are so afraid of the name "cancer" that they often refer to it as the "c" word. But cancer is just a name. We can use it to identify a specific problem. But at the same time, we must realize there is a Name that's greater, more powerful, and carries more weight than the name "cancer" or any other name in this universe. Philippians 2:10 says, "*. . . at the name of Jesus EVERY knee should bow, of those in heaven, and of those on earth, and of those under the earth.*"

So it doesn't matter what your giant's name is, the Name of Jesus is higher! That giant will have to bow its knee at Jesus' majestic Name!

What giant is hindering you today? Is it a giant of fear? Insecurity? Worry? Sickness? Poverty? Addiction? Unbelief? The sooner you recognize the giant that's been holding you back, the sooner you can deal with it in faith and kill that giant once and for all! You *must* identify the giant you're facing before you can ever expect to overcome it and possess the promises of God.

Don't Let the Enemy Blur Your Perspective

One of the worst things we can do when a brother or sister in Christ is facing a giant is to try to minimize or make light of the other person's problem. The problems and challenges of life are real. Giants roam the land today in the form of sickness, disease, poverty, addiction, despondency, and so forth. Some of these giants may seem insurmountable or impossible to overcome, but the things that are impossible with man are possible with God (Luke 18:27).

But what happens when the giant *isn't* real, or it is isn't as big or insurmountable as it seems? Many times, the giants in life will make themselves out to be bigger, scarier, and more powerful than they really are. Before we react to a problem or challenge, we need to maintain our composure while we pray about what to do.

Sometimes a test or trial is not really a giant; it's just a shadow that appears as a giant. The Lord could give you the wisdom to make that test or trial disappear instantly. He could tell you simply to stay calm and do nothing while you look to Him. You might find that the thing you thought was a problem in the morning could be gone by the afternoon!

Often, the devil tries to make something look bigger than it really is. As I said before, if he can get you into the arena of mental reasoning and fear, he knows he has you whipped! You cannot exercise faith and yield to fear at the same time. Certainly, you might exercise faith while fear's presence is standing at the door of your mind, ready to pounce. But that doesn't mean you're yielding to the fear or meditating on that fear-filled feeling or thought.

The Deceptive Nature of Shadows

Have you ever noticed that at certain times of the day—depending on where the earth is positioned relative to the sun or moon—an object can produce a longer shadow than usual? And that shadow can make the object look much bigger than it really is.

When I was a kid, we had thin cloth shades that covered the windows in our house. Those shades were opaque enough to keep the sun out by day, but they were sheer enough that you could see objects behind them, especially at night. The shades could be rolled up to allow the sun in, or they could be pulled down to keep the sun out or for privacy at night. At night, the moonlight or even a streetlight could cause some pretty scary shadows to appear behind those shades! To a kid alone in the dark, those shadows were an ominous sight!

How many times as a kid did you think you were seeing a man's hand slowly wave back and forth outside your window, only to discover that it was nothing more than a tree branch swaying in the breeze! You lay in bed trembling with fear over the shadow of a harmless tree!

Similarly, the devil loves it when we tremble and quake with fear over something that doesn't really exist—just a "shadow" of a giant instead of the giant itself. Shadows have a way of twisting things out of perspective. Shadows can make "mountains out of molehills" and "much ado about nothing." But the reactions they often cause can be potentially devastating.

For example, think of the trouble that could come from acting on the "shadow" or lie that everyone at your job hates you. If you entertain that thought and yield to it, pretty soon someone will unintentionally say or do something that completely "sets you off." You will have reacted to a shadow—to an unclear, distorted image—not the truth.

I once read a story about a man who awakened one night and, looking through his bedroom window, saw in the dim moonlight a shadowy figure moving toward his house. The figure would take a few steps backward and then proceed toward the house again.

Fully awake, adrenaline pumping throughout the man's body, he grabbed a shotgun from his closet, opened the back door, and shot at the menacing figure. The man emptied every shell from his rifle—and the ghostly figure continued to move!

Hearing the shots, the man's wife was awakened and ran to the door, screaming angrily. Her husband had just shot her best dress full of holes as it hung on the clothesline to dry!

That's a humorous story, but the things we fear in life—even if they are imagined—are not funny. In fact, these images made by "smoke and mirrors," although they're nothing more than someone's misperceptions, can ruin people's lives. We must learn to yield and hold steadfast to the truth of God's Word. Only then will we be able to navigate through the shadows that can rob us of our focus and cause us to lose our way in life.

Identify the Strengths and Weaknesses of Your Giant

If you want to become a giant killer, you must identify the strengths and weaknesses of your giant. Second Corinthians 2:11 says, "*. . . lest Satan should take advantage of us; for we are not* *ignorant of his devices."* Our Enemy, Satan, will gain the advantage over us in life if we are ignorant of his schemes—of his *modus operandi*, or "mode of operation." The only way we're going recognize his schemes and successfully stand against them is through our knowledge of God's Word and our identity with Christ and His Holy Spirit—the "Giant" inside each one of us.

That is why I emphasize so strongly the importance of reading, studying, and meditating on the Word of God as the key to living a victorious Christian life. If we fail to develop this discipline, we will find ourselves at a loss when we're confronted by giants.

To illustrate this truth, any serious coach knows that if he wants to win, he must identify the strengths and weaknesses of the opposing team. Therefore, he will watch hours of game films to identify a rival's favorite plays and best players, as well as their weak spots—their Achilles' heel. In preparing for a big game, the coach uses what he learns to fortify his own team against the opponent's strengths and also to exploit the opponent's weaknesses.

Notice that when a sports team "attacks" another team, they don't attack at the other team's strongest point. Instead, they take advantage of them at their weakest point, their point of vulnerability. Similarly, you must know the Enemy's strengths and weaknesses as well as your own strengths and weaknesses. You need to play to your strengths and shore up your weaknesses against Satan's attacks.

As I said previously, the Enemy's primary strength lies in his ability to deceive and to distract and lure you away from the Word of God and the realm of faith. If he can get you to begin to doubt God's Word or to reason away your faith, he will defeat you handily. But when you "hold" the Enemy in the realm of faith and believing—declaring without wavering, *"It is written"*—he is no match for you and the mighty strength and power of God's Word.

Identify Your Spiritual Weapons

Remember, Jesus said in John 15:5, *". . . 'without Me you can do nothing.'"* That means that apart from Jesus, the Living Word, you will be at a loss facing off with the giants of life. So the next thing you must do to become a giant killer is to identify your spiritual weapons.

Ephesians 6:10–18 enumerates our spiritual arsenal, and every one of those pieces of armor or weaponry is vitally connected to the Word of God. For example, verse 17 says, *"And take . . . the sword of the Spirit, which is the word of God. . . ."*

We know that the Word of God becomes a powerful force when it is planted deep in our hearts and then spoken from our own mouths in faith. But it's not speaking just *any* scripture that will produce the power to overcome our giants. It's speaking the *right* scripture that will get the job done.

I can't count how many times over the years I've seen people with real needs, facing real giants, who had no spiritual weaponry or ammunition in their arsenal to take care of the need. For example, I have seen those who needed healing spend all of their time studying the Word of God on the subject of end-time events. They were well-versed in the study of eschatology, but they couldn't quote a single verse on healing from memory!

The Apostle Paul wrote to the Corinthian church about the importance of believing and then speaking what you believe: "... *we have the same spirit of faith, according to what is written, 'I believed and therefore I spoke,' we also BELIEVE and therefore SPEAK...*" (2 Cor. 4:13).

And most of us are familiar with what Jesus said concerning believing and speaking.

MARK 11:23 (KJV)

23 For verily I say unto you, That whosoever shall say unto this mountain, Be thou removed, and be thou cast into the sea; and shall not doubt in his heart, but shall believe that those things which he saith shall come to pass; he shall have whatsoever he saith.

So we know that the principle of "believing and speaking" is important. But equally important is *what* we're believing and speaking. In other words, believing and speaking, "By His stripes, I'm healed" (1 Peter 2:24) is going to be of little help to you if you're in desperate need of finances!

To illustrate this point, suppose you had a .30-caliber rifle, but all you had for ammunition were 20-millimeter cannon shells. Those cannon shells are powerful, but they won't work in your rifle. For all intents and purposes, you might as well not even have a weapon! You need the right ammunition—the right scripture—to use with your weapon of "believing and speaking" God's Word!

The Right Weapon for Each Confrontation

Sometimes Christians want to have a long prayer meeting about something they're going through when they should be exercising their God-given authority in the situation. For example, if you need some extra money to meet your obligations, you might not need to have a prayer meeting. Instead, you may need to command Satan to take his hands off your money and then send out the ministering spirits—angels—to bring in the money you need (see Luke 10:19; Heb. 1:14). You may need to tell those ministering spirits, "In Jesus' Name, go and cause the money to come."

Or you may need to simply stand in faith on Philippians 4:19 or some other scripture along the same line. Instead of praying for hours on end, you may need to simply plant your feet on the Word and declare, "My God shall supply all my need according to His riches in glory!"

Don't misunderstand me. I'm not against prayer. Prayer is powerful, and we should be doing more of it! But sometimes we don't need long hours of prayer. We simply need to step out in faith and do what we know to do. David didn't have a prayer meeting before he went out to face Goliath. David no doubt lived a life of prayer while he was out tending his father's sheep. And God didn't call the Israelites to have a prayer meeting before going into the Promised Land. He simply laid out the plan and instructed them to obey Him and stick with the plan.

So I'm not against prayer. Prayer plays a vital role in the life of the believer. We need a strong prayer life to maintain our spiritual walk with God and to stay attuned to His Spirit. However, all the praying in the world cannot take the place of obedience—of stepping out in faith and acting on what God has already said in His Word.

Activate Your Weapons!

It's one thing to read, study, and meditate on the Word of God until your heart is filled with the truth of God's Word. But the Word that remains unspoken in your heart will not be effectual against the giants that come against you in life.

So the next thing you must do to become a giant killer is to *activate* your weapons! The devil is no match for the giant-killing believer who has a full arsenal of spiritual weaponry and then actively uses that weaponry to defeat the giant in his or her life.

Loaded With Faith, Yet Powerless in Battle

When I was in the U.S. Army, I trained with an M-1 rifle, a semiautomatic, gas-operated weapon. Over the course of our training, we had to learn everything there was to know about that rifle; we had to know it inside and out. We had to know how to clean it, load it, and most importantly, fire it.

To load an M-1, you had to pop a bolt before you snapped in the clip. But you had to release the bolt before a shell could enter the chamber. That means you could actually snap in a clip filled with eight .30-caliber shells, lock it down, and still be unable to fire a single shot! In other words, you could have a weapon—one that's fully loaded—but it's completely useless if it isn't properly activated!

You see, it's not enough just to have a weapon. You must know how to *activate* that weapon so you can use it. In the same way, it's not enough for us just to have faith. We must learn to activate our faith against the giants of life. We must develop a "spirit of faith" that believes God's Word and then speaks it!

My father left me a legacy of faith because he continually lived a life of faith. Like Caleb, my dad "followed the Lord fully" (Num. 14:24), defeating giants and possessing the promises of God in the face of incredible odds. What he taught from the pulpit and through his teaching materials, he lived every day of his life.

You were born to be a giant killer. And you, too, can leave a legacy of faith to your children and their children. No giant in this life is any match for you when you learn to activate your spiritual weaponry and use your faith by believing and speaking God's Word. You can become a giant killer, confronting your giants and watching them fall before you, utterly destroyed by your bold, continual confession of God's Word!

Chapter 8

CHARACTERISTICS OF A GIANT KILLER

We've seen that troublesome times come to all of us. And we know that God has given every believer the ability to obtain the victory in the midst of trouble. He has given every one of us the ability to be a giant killer—to stand successfully against spiritual opposition and receive our promised blessing. But not everyone will walk in victory in the midst of trouble and come out on "the other side" victorious. Not everyone will answer the call to be a giant killer, because being a giant killer requires a deep commitment to God and His Word.

Being a giant killer comes with its own share of challenges. For example, when you're a giant killer, there will always be someone to criticize you for stepping out in faith. People might call you arrogant, overconfident, or self-righteous. They may taunt you because of your zeal, calling you fanatical or just plain crazy!

If you want to be a giant killer, there's a price to be paid. But the rewards of slaying giants and winning victories will far outweigh the cost. In this chapter, we're going to look at some of the characteristics of a giant killer by studying David's defeat of Goliath. Hopefully, these characteristics will help you identify yourself or show you the areas you need to develop so that you can become a more successful giant killer.

A Giant Killer Is Undistracted
by Criticism or Persecution

It's important to remember that when you're a giant killer, there will always be someone to criticize you for stepping out in faith to obtain the promises of God. Let's look at the criticism and persecution David faced from his own brother before he ever stepped out to face his giant, Goliath.

1 SAMUEL 17:26-28

26 Then David spoke to the men who stood by him, saying, "What shall be done for the man who kills this Philistine and takes away the reproach from Israel? For who is this uncircumcised Philistine, that he should defy the armies of the living God?"

27 And the people answered him in this manner, saying, "So shall it be done for the man who kills him."

28 Now Eliab his oldest brother heard when he spoke to the men; and ELIAB'S ANGER WAS AROUSED AGAINST DAVID, and he said, "Why did you come down here? And with whom have you left those few sheep in the wilderness? I know your pride and the insolence of your heart, for you have come down to see the battle."

Eliab criticized and belittled his brother David because David had the heart of a giant killer. Verse 28 says. "... *Eliab's anger was aroused against David....*"

Has anyone ever become angry with you because of your faith in God? Perhaps the person who became angry or criticized you was convicted about his own lack of commitment to follow through on receiving God's promises. Or maybe the person simply didn't understand you. As my father used to say, whatever people aren't "up" on, they're usually "down" on! It's easy for people to criticize something they don't understand. So if you desire to be a giant killer, be prepared to have people talk against you or make fun of you—even some of your closest friends or relatives.

Notice what David did after Eliab mocked and ridiculed him.

1 SAMUEL 17:29-30

29 And David said, "What have I done now? Is there not a cause?"

30 Then he turned from him toward another and said the same thing; and these people answered him as the first ones did.

Notice David didn't try to defend his curiosity. He didn't try to preach Eliab a sermon. David simply said, "What have I done wrong? Can't I speak? Can't I ask a question?"

The next thing David did is significant. It says he turned his back on Eliab! When Eliab began to criticize David, he simply did an about-face and continued asking others about the Philistine who had defied the armies of Israel. You may have to turn your back on your critics too. Instead of trying to change their minds, you may just have to walk away.

Some people become distracted from destroying their giant and receiving their promise because someone criticized them. But not David. Although his older brother Eliab treated him with disdain, David simply turned around, undistracted, and continued asking questions: "What about this Philistine giant? Who does he think he is, anyway? What will the man get who kills him?"

WHERE IS GOD IN MY STORM?

A Giant Killer Is Confident and Doesn't Waver or Doubt

After David asked repeated questions about the Philistine giant and the promised rewards for killing him, someone alerted King Saul. And Saul called for David.

1 SAMUEL 17:31–32

31 Now when the words which David spoke were heard, they reported them to Saul; and he sent for him.

32 Then David said to Saul, "Let no man's heart fail because of him; your servant will go and fight with this Philistine."

Notice David didn't say to Saul, "Well, uh, let's see . . . uh . . . I guess I could go out there and try to take care of this giant. I'll see what I can do." No, David said, in effect, "Hey, don't you guys be upset! I'll handle it!

David's actions remind me of the actions of a certain quarterback at Garland High School in the early 1960s. In the fall of 1963, Garland High was playing its last game for the state championship in their league. The other team was ahead with only one minute and two seconds left on the clock. Garland had gained possession of the ball at their own 20-yard line. This quarterback ran into the huddle from the sideline, and as the story goes, he got down on one knee and rallied his players, saying, "Never fear—Jimmy's here! Okay guys, here's what we're going to do. . . ." And Jimmy proceeded to call a few plays and formations. Then he said, "Let's go!"

In less than one minute and two seconds, Garland High advanced down the field and scored the winning touchdown, winning the state title! Garland was the underdog in that game; the other team had been highly favored to win. But the tremendous confidence of that quarterback sparked confidence among his teammates. And it caused them to emerge victorious as a result.

Now, I'm certain there were those who were offended at Jimmy's confidence in his abilities and his team's abilities. But there were many others who were grateful for this young man's strong leadership! Jimmy was unwavering in his commitment to win. He refused to doubt even when the chips were down and time was running out.

Jimmy had confidence in his natural abilities, but David was supremely confident in God and *His* great ability and power! And that's the kind of unwavering confidence you need if you're going to be a giant killer.

A Giant Killer Is Not a Copycat

Too many times we try to achieve success in life by doing something we have seen someone else do. Churches do it all the time. A pastor sees a certain program that's working in another church, so he institutes the same program in his church. But doing that doesn't always work. A pastor or ministry leader needs to find out what God would have him do and then do that instead of simply copying what someone else is doing.

Saul wanted David to fight the giant the way Saul would have fought him—with a full suit of armor and the weapons of a man of war. Really, King Saul didn't have much confidence in this young shepherd boy.

1 SAMUEL 17:33-39

33 And Saul said to David, "You are not able to go against this Philistine to fight with him; for you are a youth, and he a man of war from his youth."

34 But David said to Saul, "Your servant used to keep his father's sheep, and when a lion or a bear came and took a lamb out of the flock,

35 I went out after it and struck it, and delivered the lamb from its mouth; and when it arose against me, I caught it by its beard, and struck and killed it.

36 Your servant has killed both lion and bear; and this uncircumcised Philistine will be like one of them, seeing he has defied the armies of the living God."

37 Moreover David said, "The Lord, who delivered me from the paw of the lion and from the paw of the bear, He will deliver me from the hand of this Philistine." And Saul said to David, "Go, and the Lord be with you!"

38 So Saul clothed David with his armor, and he put a bronze helmet on his head; he also clothed him with a coat of mail.

39 David fastened his sword to his armor and tried to walk, for he had not tested them. And David said to Saul, "I cannot walk with these, for I have not tested them." So David took them off.

First, I want you to notice from this passage that David was already prepared to square off with the giant because of his past experiences of trusting God. He didn't volunteer to face the giant based on what he'd heard about God or based on someone else's experience with God. David had his own experiences with God.

Similarly, if you're going to be a giant killer, you must have a personal commitment to God and His Word. You can't face off against the giants in life based on the faith of your spouse, your parents, your pastor, or your friends. It's what you know and believe about God's Word—and what you're willing to act on— that will put you over the top in life.

I also want you to notice that after Saul agreed to let David fight Goliath, Saul put his own armor on the young warrior. But when David awkwardly tried to walk in Saul's armor, he realized that it didn't fit quite right. He had never tested, or proved, the king's armor.

Have you ever heard a teenager say about some article of clothing, "I can't wear this; it just isn't 'me'"? David said almost the same thing about wearing Saul's armor. Saul's armor made him uncomfortable, so he took it off. David didn't try to be something he wasn't.

In our own lives, it's important that we not try to copy the faith of someone else. Certainly, we're supposed to fellowship with those of like faith, and we can be inspired by someone else's faith and manner of living. But God expects us to walk with Him personally. He wants us to develop ourselves—spirit, soul, and body— according to His plan and the call that's on *our* life.

He doesn't want you to try to be someone else, even if that other person is a "king" or someone of great importance. When you try to fit into the mold of someone else's life, you'll fail to properly identify with what God has for your own life.

Faith Can't Be Faked!

People in what some call the "word of faith" movement talk a lot about the confession of God's Word. And it is good and right to continually keep the confession of God's Word on our lips. But our confession of God's Word should be a confession of our hearts, not just of our heads. In other words, our confession of faith in God's Word should be personal and real to us, not just a "recording" of what we heard someone else say.

As the pastor of a large church, the leader of an international ministry, and the head of a ministry training center, I have seen people do some things, not out of faith, but because they were copying what someone else did. For example, I've heard wonderful testimonies of how the Lord led certain people to sow something into someone else's life, and God supernaturally blessed them far beyond the measure of the seed they had sown. Then some well-meaning Christians heard those testimonies and decided they would try it too. So they gave away something significant, but nothing happened. They became upset because they thought God had failed them. But He never told them to give the gift in the first place!

For example, I once heard a student at our training center share how the Lord led him to give away a car. He obeyed what he heard the Lord say, and not long afterward, someone blessed this student with a brand-new automobile! Another student heard that testimony and decided he would give away his car too. But at the end of the school year, this student was still on foot!

This young man had unwisely given away his only vehicle. The Lord didn't tell him to do it; he just did it because he was copying someone else. It's not that this man didn't have any faith. He simply tried to act on the faith and obedience of someone else instead of on what God was telling him to do personally.

I'm not saying that we have to have a word from God before we give something away. God wants us to give, but He wants us to do it from our hearts. The Bible says that God loves a cheerful giver (2 Cor. 9:7). And we shouldn't give just to get something in return. However, when God specifically leads us to sow a seed—as He did when he told that first student to give away his car—we can be confident that He already has a plan to multiply that seed sown and bless our faith and obedience in giving (2 Cor. 9:10).

God is no respecter of persons (Acts 10:34). What He does for one, He will do for another. But in receiving from God, a person's faith is involved. He has to know the level of his own faith and not try to go beyond that. He has to go to battle wearing his own armor and use the weaponry that he knows will work for him.

A giant killer will not copycat the faith or actions of others. A giant killer knows who he is and where he is going in life. He's not concerned with what the next person is doing. He has his eyes squarely on Jesus and His Word.

A Giant Killer Is Faithful

David didn't just wake up one day and say, "I think I'll do some great exploit for God." No, God prepared David in the small things before He brought him face to face with the giant.

David proved his faithfulness in the small things as he shepherded his father's flocks. It was a job David took seriously, because when a lion or bear came to threaten the safety of the sheep, David killed the predator, defending the livestock in his care.

Some Christians have a careless attitude toward their job. They want to be successful in life, but they don't want to do what it takes to get there. But God is looking for faithfulness. Luke 16:12 says, ". . . *'if you have not been faithful in what is another man's, who will give you what is your own?'* "

It wasn't David's destiny to tend sheep for the rest of his life. But while he was in charge of his father's flocks, David was serious about his responsibilities. In the same way, if we're going to be giant killers, we must practice faithfulness in everything we do.

Success takes time and effort; it doesn't happen overnight. Many young people aspire to sign professional sports contracts. But few of them realize the sacrifice and dedication it will take to achieve their aspirations. Others have other admirable goals, but those goals will only be realized if they practice faithfulness in the little things.

I know a man who served as the graduate assistant coach at the University of Iowa when B. J. Armstrong was a student there. This man related that B. J. Armstrong would stay late at the gym on weekends to practice passing and shooting. In fact, the assistant coach would help him, making thousands of passes to the young player so he could work on his long-distance shooting.

Someone once made a comment to B. J. Armstrong that he should take a Friday night off and go out to relax and have fun. The young college player responded, "When I get to the NBA, I might go out on a Friday night. But right now, I'm doing what it takes to get there."

B. J. Armstrong was the all-time leader in assists at the University of Iowa and went on to play for the Chicago Bulls, where he enjoyed an illustrious career. He was the third leading scorer in the 1993-94 season. In the previous season, he claimed the NBA's three-point field-goal percentage crown with a mark of .453.

Someone might look at B. J. Armstrong's life and say, "He was so lucky to have played professional basketball." But his success was no mere coincidence. No, B. J. Armstrong was *faithful*, and his diligence and dedication paid off in the long run.

A person could also be faithful or unfaithful in his attitude toward the Word of God. Faithfulness means being a doer of the Word (James 1:23) even when you don't feel like it. If you're faithful and determined to see the manifestation of something you're believing for, the moment you think about that promised blessing, you'll lift your hands in praise to God for what He's doing—even while you don't see a thing happening, in the natural. And if a thought crosses your mind that you're not going to get what you prayed for, you'll jump on that thought with the Word of God and take that thought captive. You'll make your thoughts come in line with the Word (2 Cor. 10:5).

I remember my dad telling a story of when he first learned to cast all of his care on the Lord. Something had happened that he was tempted to worry about. But he had learned the verse in First Peter 5:7 that talks about casting our cares on the Lord. When the temptation to worry came, he stopped and said, in effect, "No, I won't take that worry. I cast that care on You, God. Now it's Your problem, not mine."

Dad related that it was difficult at first. He had grown up a "world-champion worrier," as he described it. At first, there were many times in the night when the temptation to worry would come. Dad would get out of bed, kneel down on the floor, and say, "Lord, I'm not taking this care. I've cast it on You, and I'm not taking it back."

Dad would do that over and over—day and night—until it became easy to "cast the care" of that situation on God. And God always took care of it, because my father was faithful to the Word of God and the things of God.

Proverbs 28:20 says, *"A faithful man will abound with blessings. . . ."* What about us today? Are we faithful to our families, our jobs, and our churches? Are we faithful in our giving, or do we just give sporadically—here and there when we feel like it? Are we faithful to assemble ourselves together as the Word commands (Heb. 10:25), or are we hit-and-miss in our church attendance?

Friend, you can't have "church" in your living room with a television or CD player and expect to be a giant killer. God wouldn't tell us to "forsake not the assembling of ourselves together" as a local church body if it wasn't important.

We must be faithful to obey the whole counsel of God—not just our favorite scriptures—if we want to obtain God's promises! And we must be undaunted by criticism, confident in the Lord, and refuse to be a copycat if we want to rise up triumphant over the giants of life!

⸺⸻

Chapter 9

A GIANT KILLER OBEYS THE WORD

A Giant Killer Is Continually Growing Spiritually

What we do with the Word of God will determine our spiritual growth as Christians. It seems that those who are faithful to act on the Word and obey it are the ones who grow up spiritually to become giant killers.

Some people accept Christ, and that's as far as they ever go with the Lord. They're battered and defeated by the storms of life. They may love God, but they haven't taken one step beyond spiritual babyhood, and they are unequipped to face the giants that stand between them and the life God intends for them to live.

Just as a baby is born and grows up naturally, we need to grow up spiritually. As Christians, we must walk with our Heavenly Father continually, and we must esteem His Word as our lifeline, so to speak. Remember, Jesus, the Living Word, said, "Apart from Me, you can do nothing" (see John 15:5).

We must never allow ourselves to grow stagnant spiritually. We must keep moving forward with God, gaining new ground and obtaining new promises. And we must help others grow spiritually along the way. Far too many who have been "in the faith" for many years become critical of others who haven't attained to their spiritual stature. But Luke 12:48 says, *"For everyone to whom much is given, from him much will be required; and to whom much has been committed, of him they will ask the more."* Instead of judging others, we need to be mindful to do what we know to do and to teach others with a spirit of patience and gentleness (2 Tim. 2:24).

Some people are ignorant of the fact that they need to grow up spiritually. Others refuse to grow spiritually because they don't want God to require anything of them. They're paying a big price for their lack of growth, because ignorance is not bliss when it comes to spiritual things. For many, ignorance will be no excuse when they stand before God to give an account of what they did with their lives and with the new life in Christ that He gave them.

The devil will take advantage of us if we're not in a position spiritually to withstand him. Even a baby Christian knows to run to God when trouble comes. But those who have refused to grow spiritually cannot claim ignorance when the storms of adversity begin to blow and the giants array themselves against them. They are called to grow spiritually, just as all are who have given their hearts to the Lord.

A Giant Killer Gives of Himself to Bless Others

When someone is in need, it's often easy to pat him on the back and comfort him by saying that God will meet the need—or even to pray for the need to be met. Certainly, we're supposed to pray for others. But the Word of God teaches us that if we have the

wherewithal to help someone in need, we're supposed to help—
not turn a deaf ear and wait for someone else to rise to the task.

1 JOHN 3:16–18

16 By this we know love, because He laid down His life for us. And we also ought to lay down our lives for the brethren.

17 But whoever has this world's goods, and sees his brother in need, and shuts up his heart from him, how does the love of God abide in him?

18 My little children, let us not love in word or in tongue, but in deed and in truth.

This passage is talking about loving fellow believers in "deed and truth," not just in words. Sometimes people don't need just another pat on the back or a scripture quoted to them as much as they need something to eat! If we want to be giant killers, we must extend the hand of blessing to bring comfort to others.

In the following passage, we will see how David was used to bring comfort to Saul, even before David faced the giant, Goliath.

1 SAMUEL 16:14–23 (NIV)

14 Now the Spirit of the Lord had departed from Saul, and an evil spirit from the Lord tormented him.

15 Saul's attendants said to him, "See, an evil spirit from God is tormenting you.

16 Let our lord command his servants here to search for someone who can play the harp. He will play when the evil spirit from God comes upon you, and you will feel better."

17 So Saul said to his attendants, "Find someone who plays well and bring him to me."

18 One of the servants answered, "I have seen a son of Jesse of Bethlehem who knows how to play the harp. He is a brave man and a warrior. He speaks well and is a fine-looking man. And the Lord is with him."

19 Then Saul sent messengers to Jesse and said, "Send me your son David, who is with the sheep."

20 So Jesse took a donkey loaded with bread, a skin of wine and a young goat and sent them with his son David to Saul.

21 David came to Saul and entered his service. Saul liked him very much, and David became one of his armor-bearers.

22 Then Saul sent word to Jesse, saying, "Allow David to remain in my service, for I am pleased with him."

23 Whenever the spirit from God came upon Saul, David would take his harp and play. Then relief would come to Saul; he would feel better, and the evil spirit would leave him.

When King Saul experienced a need to be comforted, one of his attendants said to him, "David's the man you want!" The servant knew of David's reputation and was able to recommend him for service to the king. The servant said about David, ". . . *'I have seen a son of Jesse of Bethlehem who knows how to play the harp. He is a brave man and a warrior. He speaks well and is a fine-looking man. AND THE LORD IS WITH HIM'"* (v. 18).

David's reputation had become well known, and he was chosen for the job of bringing comfort to the king in his distress. Similarly, when you have an outstanding reputation for being gifted in some area and blessing others with your gift, you will be promoted, just as David was promoted to the position of armor-bearer for the king.

When a pastor or ministry leader today looks for paid or volunteer staff to assist him in the work of the ministry, he often depends on word-of-mouth recommendations similar to the recommendation the attendant made to King Saul. There have been times when we've needed to fill a certain position at our ministry, and one of my staff has said, "Hey, what about so-and-so?" because that staff member had noticed how the person was always blessing others with his gifts and talents.

Most of the promotions that people receive in the workplace happen because those people had established a reputation for being a blessing to the corporation or place of business they worked for. I encourage you to ask yourself the questions, "When people look at me, do they recognize that 'the Lord is with me'? Do they see me developed in my skill or trade? Do they see in me a generous and meek spirit that's willing to give instead of always asking, 'What's in it for me' "?

When you bless others, you encourage them and lift them up. You provide words of comfort, and you *become* a blessing. So many Christians today are more concerned with being blessed than with being a blessing. But to be a successful giant killer, you must focus on blessing others.

Growing up in my parents' home, I never once heard my father pray, "Lord, bless me." Instead, he always prayed, "Lord, make me a blessing." Yet how many people do we know of today who would pray more along the line, "Lord, bless me and my wife and kids—*us four and no more*"!

Certainly, there's nothing wrong with asking God for things. But there's a time for doing that, and there's also a time for seeking opportunities to give and to bless others. Often people lose their perspective and spend all of their time focusing on themselves and their own needs. But God is raising up a generation of giant killers who are looking for opportunities to put others first and to be the blessing God intended for them to be.

A Giant Killer Is Courageous

In First Chronicles 28:20 King David said to his son Solomon, ". . . *'Be strong and of good courage. . . .'*" Why did he say that? Because he knew if Solomon was going to be a giant killer—if he was going to be successful in facing the challenges of life—he had to be a person of courage.

Fear is a deadly enemy to your faith and your spiritual walk. You're going to have to banish it from your life if you expect to slay giants and live victoriously.

Notice the characteristics of courage and boldness in David's life when he was just a youth tending his father's sheep.

1 SAMUEL 17:34-35

34 But David said to Saul, "Your servant used to keep his father's sheep, and when a lion or a bear came and took a lamb out of the flock,

35 I went out after it and struck it, and delivered the lamb from its mouth; and when it arose against me, I caught it by its beard, and struck and killed it.

David wasn't making this up! He rehearsed before Saul, "When a lion or bear stole a lamb from my father's flock, I went after that wild animal. I took back my lamb. And when the lion or bear rose up against me, I caught it by the fur and killed it!"

David refused to fear! And if you want to be a giant killer, you're going to have to take the same attitude toward the Enemy. If Satan has stolen something from you, you need to say, like David, "You can't have that! I want it back!" By faith, you need to take back what belongs to you—your health, your finances, and so forth. And if the Enemy rises up to protest, you're going to have to strike him hard with the sword of God's Word!

David possessed this godly characteristic of courage. Notice that after he rehearsed to Saul his experiences with the wild animals that preyed on his livestock, David added, *"'Your servant has killed both lion and bear; and this uncircumcised Philistine will be like one of them, seeing he has defied the armies of the living God'"* (1 Sam. 17:36)!

Then notice that after David was sent out to face Goliath, David didn't wait for the giant to draw his weapon.

1 SAMUEL 17:48

48 So it was, when the Philistine arose and came and drew near to meet David, that DAVID HURRIED AND RAN TOWARD THE ARMY TO MEET THE PHILISTINE.

Many times believers will wait until some giant is looming ferociously over them before they'll draw their weapons. For example, instead of jumping on the first sign of a symptom in their bodies with Word of God, they'll wait until the doctors have given them a bad report. Or instead of jumping on a small decrease in their finances with God's Word, they'll wait until the bottom has fallen out, so to speak, and the situation is dire.

To be a giant killer, you must have the courage and initiative to face the challenger at the first sign of a challenge! Don't take the attitude, *Well, we'll just wait to see how everything goes.* Be aggressive with the Word of God in your heart and mouth, and give the devil no place to "set up shop" or take any territory where your life is concerned.

I like to get up every morning and say, "Glory to God, by Jesus' stripes, I am healed! He took from me every infirmity and disease. I'm strong in the Lord and in the power of His might. I'm healed, whole, prosperous, and of a sound mind!" Every day we should continually inform ourselves and every demon and devil exactly who we are in Christ and what we have in Him.

Don't ever sit idly by, just waiting for a storm to roll into your life at full force. Keep yourself in a state of preparedness by whipping every "lion and bear" that tries to steal even the smallest blessing from you! That way, when the giants of life try to rise up and defeat you, they will be no match for the strength and fearlessness of the Holy One Who rises up inside you to fight!

A Giant Killer Finishes the Job

Notice that after David sank a stone into Goliath's forehead, knocking the giant to the ground, he didn't stop there. David made a decisive end of the giant in front of all the Philistine armies who had trusted so confidently in their warrior, Goliath.

1 SAMUEL 17:49-51

49 Then David put his hand in his bag and took out a stone; and he slung it and STRUCK THE PHILISTINE IN HIS FOREHEAD, so that the stone sank into his forehead, AND HE FELL ON HIS FACE TO THE EARTH.

50 So David prevailed over the Philistine with a sling and a stone, and struck the Philistine and killed him. BUT THERE WAS NO SWORD IN THE HAND OF DAVID.

51 THEREFORE DAVID ran and stood over the Philistine, TOOK HIS [Goliath's] SWORD and drew it out of its sheath AND KILLED HIM, AND CUT OFF HIS HEAD WITH IT. And when the Philistines saw that their champion was dead, they fled.

David the giant killer didn't stop until the job was done! Remember, the Philistine armies were poised to annihilate Israel as a nation and take their survivors captive. But when David cut off the head of their champion warrior, they lost their confidence and fled! In other words, they took off! But the armies of Israel pursued them and soundly defeated them, plundering the spoils from the enemy's camps.

Now, I don't know if David took off the giant's head just to intimidate the Philistines, to ensure that Goliath wouldn't rouse from unconsciousness and take David from behind, or to preserve the giant's head as a souvenir and token of victory! But I do know that David left those battlegrounds that day a decisive conqueror and hero.

One thing you learn in military training is never to assume in combat that your enemy is dead. In other words, a soldier must be sure his enemy is dead or taken captive. A good soldier is taught that dead soldiers can't take you from behind! So in combat, a soldier will never just assume an enemy soldier is dead and then turn his back on him and walk away.

Many a soldier and even entire troops have been taken out because the opposition "played possum" and was able to catch their enemy off guard. So don't ever turn your back on a spiritual giant and allow it to remain a threat to your life. Remember, a half-defeated giant is still a giant. As a trained, anointed giant killer, you must finish the job in every spiritual battle!

A Giant Killer Keeps a Humble Attitude

If you're going to be a giant killer, you must keep a humble attitude. James 4:6 says, ". . . *God resists the proud, But gives grace to the humble.*" Arrogance and pride have defeated many Christians who would have otherwise been champion giant killers in the Kingdom of God.

Studying the life of David, you'll find that although God anointed David and allowed him to accomplish many outstanding feats, David always acknowledged that God had given him his victories. Even after the prophet Samuel anointed David as king in Saul's stead, David never got ahead of God. He never tried to steal the kingship from Saul in his own timing and strength. Instead, David waited on the Lord and was respectful toward Saul until the end of the king's life— although Saul had tried many times to kill David.

Once as King Saul and his men were pursuing David, Saul entered a cave not knowing that David and his men were hiding inside. David cut off a piece of Saul's robe, but he didn't harm the king. Afterward, David showed Saul the patch of garment to let the king know that he had spared his life even while Saul was seeking David's life! (See 1 Sam. 24:1–15)

David maintained an honorable spirit toward Saul and walked in deep reverence before the Lord. Even later in David's life when he sinned against God with Bathsheba, David repented sorely before the Lord. And the Lord accepted David's heartfelt repentance. God even said about this giant killer, "He is a man after My own heart, who will do all of My will" (see Acts 13:22).

I have seen Christians boast and brag about their great faith, barely acknowledging the hand of God in the blessings they had received. The cure for this kind of irreverence and pride is sincere gratitude to God for every good thing in a person's life. God is not only the Giver, He's the Author of our salvation and our faith! Even our faith is the gift of God (Eph. 2:8)!

If we're going to be giant killers, we must keep a humble spirit and avoid pride, arrogance, and selfishness at all costs. We must also constantly seek to grow spiritually and give of ourselves to others. We must finish the tasks God has given us, and we must banish even the smallest hint of fear from our lives so we can complete the job that is set before us. The more we obey God's Word in every area of our lives, the more victories will be ours to enjoy as we face and *destroy* our giants!

———※———

Chapter 10

DON'T 'ABANDON SHIP'
JUST BEFORE THE SHORE!

If we want to cross over to the other side of our trials and troubles, we must learn to esteem the virtues of God's Word. But in the uncertainty of modern life, many have given up on the Word. From their point of view, the "shoreline" they've been seeking so desperately is nowhere in sight. They're about to "abandon ship" where faith is concerned.

But they have forgotten that the Word of God—the Bible—is not just a collection of words and sayings in a sacred book. God's Word, including each word that is written, is the very power of God to those who will believe it (Rom. 1:16).

How do we make this "storehouse" of power operative and effective for us personally?

HEBREWS 4:12–16

12 For the word of God is living and powerful, and sharper than any two-edged sword, piercing even to the division of soul and spirit, and of joints and marrow, and is a discerner of the thoughts and intents of the heart.

13 And there is no creature hidden from His sight, but all things are naked and open to the eyes of Him to whom we must give account.

14 Seeing then that we have a great High Priest who has passed through the heavens, Jesus the Son of God, LET US HOLD FAST OUR CONFESSION.

15 For we do not have a High Priest who cannot sympathize with our weaknesses, but was in all points tempted as we are, yet without sin.

16 Let us therefore come boldly to the throne of grace, that we may obtain mercy and find grace to help in time of need.

Notice the words in verse 12: *"The word of God is living and powerful. . . ."* Other translations read:

"The word of God is quick, and powerful . . ." (KJV).

"The word of God is living and active" (NIV).

"God's Message is full of life and power . . ." (Weymouth).

The Word of God is a living, breathing entity. It is alive and active, not passive. Have you ever heard someone say about a child, "That child is very active"? They mean the child is never still. Similarly, God's Word is always moving, pulsating with power.

The next part of verse 12 says, *". . . and sharper than any two-edged sword. . . ."* The Word of God is a spiritual force able to accomplish things that mere humans cannot. The last part of this verse tells us that the Word pierces *". . . even to the division of soul and spirit, and of joints and marrow, and is a discerner of the thoughts and intents of the heart."*

The Word of God is sharp and potent enough to separate our souls from our spirits. It shines a light upon our motives and lights a pathway on which we can walk (Ps. 119:105). The Word of God dispels darkness, reproves error, and imparts instruction (John 1:5; 2 Tim. 3:16). The Word of God is also where we can go to be strengthened, encouraged, and receive the help we need.

In times of trouble, have you ever just opened your Bible to read and found that the Lord was an ever-present help in your time of need? As you read, peace came over you and words of hope seemed to "leap" from the page? You thought you couldn't persevere through the trial you were facing. But suddenly, you sensed with renewed confidence and strength, "I can make it! And I will win!"

The Word of God will also cleanse you and preserve you from sin. The Psalmist wrote, "*Your word I have hidden in my heart, That I might not sin against You*" (Ps. 119:11). And Ephesians 5:26 says that Christ "sanctifies and cleanses" His Body, the Church, with the "washing of water by the Word."

The Word of God and every promise therein is powerful. And the Word of God in your heart and on your lips can become a life-changing force. God's Word is infallible, immutable, indestructible, eternal, and unchanging. It's a sure foundation on which you can base your faith and trust.

1 PETER 1:23–25 (NIV)

23 For you have been born again, not of perishable seed, but of IMPERISHABLE, through the LIVING AND ENDURING word of God.

24 For, "All men are like grass, and all their glory is like the flowers of the field; the grass withers and the flowers fall,

25 but the word of the Lord STANDS FOREVER." And this is the word that was preached to you.

Jesus said, *"Heaven and earth will pass away, but My words will by no means pass away"* (Luke 21:33). God's Word is not weaker today than it was in the past. Every generation since the time of Adam until the present has faced its own times of uncertainty and unrest. But God and His Word remain the same. The Word of God is as powerful today as it was when God said in the Creation, *"Let there be light,"* and light "became" (Gen. 1:3).

God said, *"I am the Lord, I change not . . ."* (Mal. 3:6 KJV). Since God "changes not," His Word "changes not," because God and His Word are one.

Hold Fast to the Unchanging Word

Do you see that the Word of God is a rock you can stand on in troubled times? When the tides of change come rolling in and fear seems to be everywhere present, God's Word is a solid, sure foundation that will not be washed away by the storm.

Someone might ask, "Reverend Hagin, do you know what's going to happen to our economy?" No, I don't know the future in detail, but I know the One Who does. I don't know what decisions are going to be made in Washington that will affect our nation and the world, but I know the One Who can change the tides to accomplish His plan and purpose. And my trust is in Him!

HEBREWS 4:14

14 Seeing then that we have a great High Priest who has passed through the heavens, Jesus the Son of God, let us hold fast our confession.

The *New International Version* says, "*. . . let us hold firmly to the faith we profess.*" When the world appears "awash" around us, that is no time to abandon ship! Instead, we must hold on tightly to Jesus, Who is with us and promised He would never leave us, forsake us, or fail us! The *Amplified Bible* says, "*. . . He [God] Himself has said, I will not in any way fail you nor give you up nor leave you without support. [I will] not, [I will] not, [I will] not in any degree leave you helpless nor forsake nor let [you] down (relax My hold on you)! [Assuredly not!]*" (Heb. 13:5).

HEBREWS 4:15-16

15 For we do not have a High Priest who cannot sympathize with our weaknesses, but was in all points tempted as we are, yet without sin.

16 Let us therefore come boldly to the throne of grace, that we may obtain mercy and find grace to help in time of need.

The difference between Christianity and other religions of the world is that the Lord is *with* us! He's not in a tomb! He's alive forevermore! And He is with us, in us, and for us! Whatever we're going through, Jesus knows about it. Because He came to earth as a man, lived a life free of sin, and died and rose on our behalf—as our Substitute for sin—He is qualified to be our faithful High Priest, Who still ministers on behalf of men who call on Him!

There is nothing you can experience in life that Jesus can't identify with. Verse 15 says He is able to sympathize with our weaknesses, because He was tempted in every way we are, yet He was without sin. He is God Almighty Who came in the flesh! And He is well qualified to help you no matter what the storm or challenge you're facing. He will help and guide you through troubled times!

Someone Is Praying for You

Not only is Jesus our High Priest, the Bible says that He is at the right hand of the Father, interceding for us.

HEBREWS 7:24–25

24 But He, because He continues forever, has an unchangeable priesthood.

25 Therefore He is also able to save to the uttermost those who come to God through Him, since He always lives to make intercession for them.

HEBREWS 7:24–25 (NIV)

24 . . . but because Jesus lives forever, he has a permanent priesthood.

25 Therefore he is able to save completely those who come to God through him, because he always lives to intercede for them.

Friend, we can have the utmost confidence in God! Jesus has gone before us as our Savior, Redeemer, and High Priest Who always intercedes on our behalf. That should embolden us to hold fast to our confession of faith in Him no matter what the storm! We can have immovable, unshakable confidence that He will steady us, strengthen us, and calm every storm. And every Word that we've held firmly to, He will bring to pass!

When the Enemy of our soul closes in and threatens us, including everything that we hold dear, we do not have to cave in or surrender to fear. We do not have to draw back and relinquish our hold on what God has promised. We don't have to abandon the command of our ship to Satan. And we don't have to "jump ship"! Jesus will be our Anchor, our steadfast hope, on the rolling tides and crashing waves. He will see us safely through the storm and guide us so that we reach our destination and receive the answer we've desired.

The Enemy will always try to shake us up so we will abandon our faith in God's ". . . *exceeding great and precious promises . . .*" (2 Peter 1:4 KJV). Satan knows that if we won't waver or quit, we will enjoy an "exceeding great reward"! That's why he constantly tries to discredit God and His Word. The Enemy brings clouds of doubt to confuse our minds so we'll waver, quit, and abandon ship. His only hope is to get us to change our minds about God's Word, because the unchanging Word of God will not fail!

A Place of Mercy

Because Jesus is our High Priest, we can hold fast to the Word of God and to our confession of faith. We can receive promises, withstand temptation, and have every area of our lives affected by the life-changing Word.

Jesus our High Priest has also provided us an open door to the Presence of God.

HEBREWS 4:14, 16

14 Seeing then that we have a great High Priest . . .

16 Let us therefore come boldly to the throne of grace, that we may obtain mercy and find grace to help in time of need.

The "throne of grace" is the Throne of God, where God sits as eternal Creator. But because of Jesus, He also sits as Everlasting Father, Whom we can approach with confidence.

Hebrews 4:16 tells us that God is a giver. But how many people who believe that God is a giver still hesitate to go to Him with their problems? They lack the boldness and confidence to approach His throne. They don't understand that because the blood of Jesus has been applied to their hearts as believers, they have free access to God's grace.

Throughout history, there have been many kings who struck fear in the hearts of their subjects. Approaching such a king for help was unthinkable. And if you ever did have to approach the king's throne, you did so with fear and trembling. In fact, in many places, you did not dare to approach a king unless you had been invited. To approach uninvited could mean death.

In the Book of Esther, we can read that Queen Esther was called upon to approach King Ahasuerus' throne without invitation. If he extended his scepter, it meant she could enter his presence. But if he *didn't* extend his scepter, it meant she would be put to death! After fasting and praying, Esther went to the king. God granted her so much favor that she saved an entire race of people who had been appointed for annihilation (see Esther 4–7).

God's throne—the throne of grace—is not a place of judgment. He is the King of kings and the only true God. His throne is a place of great mercy and favor! And God has invited us to approach Him boldly, with confidence and without fear, because of the blood of Jesus and His permanent position as our High Priest.

I have five grandsons who all know how to come boldly to me, their "Poppy." When those boys come to the ministry to visit me, I guarantee you, they aren't afraid to approach me. They know they can enter my office confidently! And it doesn't matter who's visiting me at the time. They simply run in without fear or hesitancy. Why? Because they're my grandchildren. They have a relationship with me.

Because of what Jesus did in His death, burial, and resurrection, we who have been born again have entered the family of God. We have a relationship with God the Father. We don't have to wait for Him to "give us the nod" before approaching Him. Jesus has made the way clear for us to approach Him anytime. He's never too busy, and we don't have to fear for our lives! We don't have to go to God with our heads down, feeling intimidated and unworthy. No, God's throne of grace is a place where we can go confidently to obtain mercy and receive help in our time of need.

We don't have to go to God begging and pleading for our needs to be met. We can simply go and acknowledge that He is good and that He changes not! Then we can say, "Father, I need help!" And we will get it, because God is a giver, and His throne is a place where we can receive from Him freely.

Help Is on the Way!

It's important for us to realize that after we've prayed, an apparent delay in the answer doesn't mean that God hasn't heard us. It doesn't mean that help is not on the way! Have you ever heard the expression, "Delays are not denials"? First John 5:14–15

— 129 —

says, *"Now this is the confidence that we have in Him, that if we ask anything according to His will, HE HEARS US. And IF WE KNOW THAT HE HEARS US, whatever we ask, WE KNOW THAT WE HAVE THE PETITIONS THAT WE HAVE ASKED OF HIM."*

When Daniel served King Cyrus in the Babylonian captivity of the Jews, Daniel began to fast and pray about a promise God had made to Israel that seemed long in coming. He prayed for about 21 days. After that, an angel visited Daniel and spoke the following words to him:

DANIEL 10:12–14

12 . . . "Do not fear, Daniel, for FROM THE FIRST DAY that you set your heart to understand, and to humble yourself before your God, YOUR WORDS WERE HEARD; and I have come because of your words.

13 But the prince of the kingdom of Persia withstood me twenty-one days; and behold, Michael, one of the chief princes, came to help me, for I had been left alone there with the kings of Persia.

14 Now I have come to make you understand what will happen to your people in the latter days, for the vision refers to many days yet to come."

Daniel was holding fast to the vision God had given His prophets concerning the nation of Israel. Yet after many years, the vision hadn't been fulfilled. Daniel sought the Lord about it for 21 days. When the angel finally arrived, he told Daniel that his words were heard *the first day he prayed*! The angel had been dispatched by God, but was opposed by "principalities and powers" in the heavenlies (see Eph. 6:12; Col. 2:15). But because of Daniel's steadfast faith, another angel was sent to help. And God's messenger angel broke through to Daniel with the answer.

I want to encourage you to not waver, quit, or abandon ship regarding whatever promise you're holding fast to from God's Word. Help is on the way! God's Word will not fail you if you'll refuse to give up. On the other hand, if you fail to hold fast to your confession of faith, the thing you desire from God will never become a reality.

Someone once said to me, "I've been believing God for so long!"

I encouraged this person, "Don't quit! Your faith will see you through if you won't give up! Keep standing on the rock of God's Word. It's a sure Word, and it won't let you down!"

When we fail to receive something that God has promised in His Word, it's because we didn't approach God in faith, or we abandoned our faith too soon. Remember the disciples at sea in their storm-tossed ship? Jesus calmed the storm and then asked them, "How is it that you have no faith?" (Mark 4:40). Because of the fierce circumstances, they had abandoned faith in the words Jesus had spoken: "Let us cross over to the other side" (v. 35). Those words were powerful enough to see them through any storm, but they didn't "hold fast" to those living, power-filled words.

I wonder how many people have "abandoned ship" and let go of their faith when the answer was just around the corner. In another storm, Jesus walked on the water to the disciples' ship as the disciples battled the elements. Some researchers say that particular body of water was only about four miles wide at its narrowest point. If that's true, when the storm was at its worst, the disciples could have been less than a half a mile *or even just a few yards* away from their destination!

Friend, your ship may be storm-tossed and battered, but you may be closer to land than you think! The devil may be shouting, *You'll never win!* But God has victory in store for you!

Has the Enemy convinced you that your problems are permanent and that your suffering will never end? You need to "wake up," run to the Word of God, and realize that the Lord will never leave you and that you're never out of His reach or His care. Don't abandon ship just before you reach the shore! No matter how rough the storm or uncertain the times, if we'll hold fast to our confession of faith in God's Word, every step that we take in faith will draw us closer to our promised victory!

Chapter 11

REJOICING THROUGH TROUBLED TIMES

Have you hit a "brick wall" in facing your storm, and no answer seems to be forthcoming? God has made a way for you to have victory. Your answer lies in Him. So where you place your focus and attention is of utmost importance when the heat is on and you don't know what else to do.

HABAKKUK 3:17-19

17 Though the fig tree may not blossom, Nor fruit be on the vines; Though the labor of the olive may fail, And the fields yield no food; Though the flock may be cut off from the fold, And there be no herd in the stalls—

18 Yet I will rejoice in the Lord, I will joy in the God of my salvation.

19 The Lord God is my strength; He will make my feet like deer's feet, And He will make me walk on my high hills.

Habakkuk paints a dark picture at the beginning of this passage—a picture of failed crops, lost livestock, no sustainable food supply, and little hope for the people's livelihood and well-being. Those are bleak circumstances! But Habakkuk doesn't stay focused on the problem. Instead he focuses on the Lord. He makes the choice to praise Him despite the negative circumstances that were coming upon Judah. Habakkuk's praise is an expression of deep reverence for God and of his faith and trust in Yahweh, the great "I Am."

It's easy to praise God when everything is going smoothly. But it's a challenge to praise Him when seemingly nothing is going right! That was Habakkuk's case. Perhaps you can't relate to failed fig and olive trees, but I'm sure you can relate to the company for which you work perhaps closing its doors.

Most of us can relate to economic loss—a downturn in the economy, a loss of a job, and no visible means of earning a decent living. Experiencing such losses can be devastating and draining. The stress can seem overwhelming. But God has still called us to a life of praise and rejoicing. Our praise is an expression of our love for God and of our faith and trust in Him. It creates an avenue through which He can work in our lives and bring blessing to us and glory to His Name.

The reality is that the circumstances of life are always changing. People can come and go, markets can fluctuate daily, and businesses can turn a profit one quarter and suffer losses the next. Even our bodies change daily. Whether we can see it or not, our bodies are aging every day of our lives.

Change is constantly happening all around us. But as we've seen, God's Word never changes. And if we remain focused on God's unchanging Word, we will be able to navigate the storms and the changing tides of life and emerge from them victorious.

Too many people live their lives completely dominated by the circumstances around them. In other words, if the circumstances are positive, these people are happy; if the circumstances are negative, these people are sad. They are "up one day and down the next"—riding an emotional roller coaster.

Hope for the Future

During the Great Depression of the 1930s, many people lost everything they owned—their homes, their automobiles and other valuables, and even many of their personal effects. Church attendance and the demand for Christian music increased during that period in history. Songs such as, "When We All Get to Heaven" and "Everybody Will Be Happy Over There" became popular. People had lost hope in the government, in Wall Street, in the economy, and perhaps even in the "American dream." But the hope of Heaven and eternal glory was a mainstay for many during that era.

At the time of this writing, we find ourselves in the midst of an alarming economic climate. With corporations reorganizing, businesses downsizing, foreclosures increasing, and investments consistently going sour, we need to focus on the "constants" in our own lives. Certainly, believers today have this same hope of Heaven, and we are obviously closer than ever before to the time of Jesus' return. But God has not left us without hope for our lives on this earth. Heaven is a glorious place, and we should look forward to spending eternity with the Lord. But we can also have confident hope in God's Word to change the circumstances and to cause us to walk in victory in this life.

Habakkuk said, *"Yet I will rejoice in the Lord, I will joy in the God of my salvation"* (Hab. 3:18). Habakkuk possessed a strong hope in God for a bright, prosperous future. Meanwhile, the circumstances he was seeing reflected anything but prosperity.

However, I see many believers today who are losing hope. They are worrying and wondering, *Oh, God, what are we going to do?*

Why was Habakkuk able to rejoice in the face of adversity? It had to be because of His knowledge of God. When you know the Lord—His character, nature, and abilities—you can remain steadfast and constant even when the circumstances of life are not. You can praise Him for Who He is even in troubled times, because He is the same "yesterday, today, and forever" (Heb. 13:8). In good times and bad, it is *always* appropriate to rejoice in the Lord.

Joy Anticipates the Victory

It's good to praise God for Who He is even when things go badly. But it's also good to praise God for the victory you're anticipating "on the other side" of the test or trial! That's another reason Habakkuk could praise God. Habakkuk "rejoiced in the God of his salvation" because he knew God would come to his aid and help him.

How would you respond if you didn't have the money to pay some big bill that was due, and someone walked up to you and said, "I'm going to take care of that for you." Would you look at that person with a completely expressionless face and say in an unemotional tone, "Oh, thank you"? No, you'd be happy and excited, wouldn't you!

When you're believing God for an answer to prayer, you need to "joy in the God of your salvation"! You need to act happy, excited, and grateful before you ever see the answer. He is the God of our salvation Who will supply every one of our needs. And since He never changes, He can be depended on to meet the need. No matter what test or trial we may be facing, we have every reason to rejoice!

ROMANS 8:32

32 He who did not spare His own Son, but delivered Him up for us all, how shall He not with Him also freely give us all things?

God did not withhold His only Son from us. He freely gave Him to ransom us from sin—to save us from a sinner's hell. Since God gave us His very best in sending Jesus, why do we sometimes doubt His willingness to heal us, deliver us, and meet our needs today?

God Is Our 'Stabilizer'

Sometimes when people face a crisis or trouble of some kind, they lack the knowledge they need to anchor themselves and help them stay focused on God instead of on the circumstances. Isaiah 33:6 says, *"Wisdom and knowledge shall be the stability of thy times, and strength of salvation . . ."* (KJV). A person's knowledge of God, as in the case of Habakkuk, can bring great stability during times of uncertainty.

It's easy to see why some people panic in a crisis or storm. They don't have anything to stabilize them or hold them steady. By way of illustration, aircraft are equipped with something known as a stabilizer, or *tailplane*. It provides stability while the aircraft is flying straight. The stabilizer balances the plane against the forces acting on the craft in flight. It helps guide and steady the plane in the air. Without a stabilizer, you would have disaster in motion!

God is our "Stabilizer"! But when we're focused on the storm rather than on God's Word, instead of rejoicing in times of trouble, we will become fearful, confused, shaky, or unsteady. We will begin to question God: "Why did this happen to me?"

Some people become angry with the Lord, with others, and even with themselves in times of trouble. They might question the pastor or the church, and often they fall away from the very things they need to help stabilize them in the midst of turmoil. They have yet to grasp the truth that every one of us faces troubles in life—no one is immune! God doesn't cause our troubles; God wants to deliver us out of trouble! That's why we must rejoice in the Lord through troubled times.

Habakkuk foresaw a time of trouble for Judah, but he didn't panic. He knew that the people of Judah were the people of God, and that God would never forsake or abandon them. Today, believers in Christ's finished work—those who have accepted Him as Savior—are the people of God too. And Hebrews 8:6 says that we have a new and better covenant "established on better promises" than those who lived under the Old Covenant.

Proving God's Faithfulness in Troubled Times

I remember a time when my dad was traveling as an itinerant preacher. Back in the 1940s and 1950s, traveling ministers weren't paid by check when they visited churches to hold a meeting. The churches simply took up an offering and gave it to the guest speaker—nickels, dimes, and all!

During this time, Dad visited a particular church where most of the members were farmers. When it was time to take up the offering, the pastor got up and made a long "pull" for money, saying, "I know it's been a bad year for the crops." You see, hail had destroyed the tomatoes in the area, and boll weevils had destroyed acres of cotton crops.

The pastor continued, "But we need to take up a good offering for Brother Hagin." Then the pastor went on for several minutes talking about the offering.

I was with Dad in that meeting. I was about nine years old at the time, and I remember it vividly. Dad had just received some revelation from the Word about prosperity, and the Lord had told my father, "Don't pray about money the way you have in the past." Then He taught Dad how to claim his needs met on the authority of the Word.

Before the next service in that meeting, Dad pulled the pastor aside and said, "Don't make any pulls for money when you take up the offering for me. Simply say, 'We're going to take up Brother Hagin's offering.' That's all I want you to say."

The pastor was astounded! He said, "Why, if I do that, you won't get a dime!"

That pastor probably thought Dad had lost his mind! But my father had discovered the greatest stabilizing force in the universe—the Word of God! And Dad was putting what he had learned to the test. In fact, he was so confident that the Lord would take care of him that he told that pastor, "Well, if all I get is a dime, you won't hear me complain or say a word about it."

Reluctantly, the pastor did what my dad had instructed him to do. The offering that night was the biggest offering the church had ever given any visiting minister! The pastor said to my dad, "That beats anything I've ever seen!"

My father didn't just teach people that they should trust God and His Word—Dad *lived* it! When the circumstances looked hopeless, he had a stabilizing force within him that held him steady through the crises of life and brought him safely to the other side of the storms in victory!

In Habakkuk 3:17–19, the prophet was telling people not to dwell on the negative circumstances but to rejoice in the Lord and keep their hearts fixed and "stabilized" on Him. Circumstances change, but God never changes! And He is our salvation. That means whatever we need—deliverance, protection, well-being, or prosperity—God can give us!

But someone might say, "You just don't understand what I'm going through!" I've heard this many times from many people in my 50 years of ministry.

Some people become offended when you try to teach them to place their focus on God in the storms of life. But encouraging someone to focus on God in a crisis isn't making light of the crisis. It's the key to getting that person *through* the crisis so they can enjoy better days ahead!

God will never override our wills. In other words, we must invite Him into our lives and into the circumstances we're facing. When we worry, fret, and complain during a test or trial, we tie God's hands, so to speak, and He isn't able to help us. We "shut the door" on God. But when we raise our hands and our voices in praise, abandoning the care and control of our problems to the Lord, we throw the door wide open for Him to come in and steady us, strengthen us, and guide us out of our troubles!

Habakkuk said, *"THE LORD GOD IS MY STRENGTH, and he will make my feet like hinds' feet, and he will make me to walk upon mine high places"* (Hab. 3:19 KJV). Some people don't want to be strengthened during a test or trial. They just want to be delivered out of the trial! They don't want God to enable them to walk on the "high places" or the difficult places in life. They just want Him to remove those difficult places *right now*! It's almost as if they want to be delivered *their* way or *no* way!

In a time of trouble, God will strengthen and enable us to come through that difficulty victoriously. He might calm our storm, or He might propel us through the storm until we reach shore. Either way, He will always cause us to triumph in Christ Jesus (2 Cor. 2:14)!

Why We Need the Strength of God

Have you ever experienced troubles and immediately looked to God concerning the situation, yet still felt as if your strength had been sapped?

We are human, and we cannot sustain ourselves in spiritual battle. When we become battered by the storms of life, we need the supernatural strength of God to sustain us. Habakkuk said, "... *he will make my feet like hinds' feet* ..." (Hab. 3:19 KJV).

When you're going through a crisis, sometimes you can feel "heavy"—bogged down by the weight of the circumstances. But have you ever seen a deer run? They are light on their feet. Deer can be standing still and then suddenly jump several feet straight into the air!

Deer are also quick. They are so graceful as they run, and they have the natural ability to dart quickly through the woods, moving with great agility and speed through tight places where the underbrush is dense.

In times of testing and trouble, God can make you like a deer. You may start out feeling like you're trudging uphill in mud and mire, but God can make you feel as if your feet are barely touching the ground!

God's Strength Fortifies You Against Fear

The psalmist David knew something about experiencing God's supernatural strength and salvation, or delivering power.

PSALM 27:1

1   The Lord is my light and my salvation; Whom shall I fear? The Lord is the strength of my life; Of whom shall I be afraid?"

The strength of God within you will fortify you against the presence of fear. Notice David said, "The Lord is my strength—of whom shall I be afraid?" We need the strength of God to walk by faith in the midst of trying times, because fear can nullify our faith and hinder our deliverance and blessing.

In the midst of trials, God can make your feet like the feet of a deer, swift and graceful. He can enable you to run your spiritual race with strength and excellence. He can cause you to fulfill your destiny, stepping into blessings you never imagined and walking in places you've never walked before.

Joy and Rejoicing—The Key to Reaping

Does your answer seem long in coming? Has God given you a vision of victory, but you have yet to see it fulfilled? I can tell you what to do to reach your intended destination and experience the reality of your promised blessing: *rejoice in the Lord!*

Remember, Habakkuk rejoiced while the situation seemed dark and hopeless. Similarly, we are called to rejoice in the Lord always—in the good times and the bad. He wants us to praise Him when things are going great and when we're still anticipating a change in our storm or crisis.

PHILIPPIANS 4:4

4 Rejoice in the Lord ALWAYS. Again I will say, rejoice!

What does victory look like to you? Does it look like a healed body? An increase in finances? A wayward child turning his life around? The children of Israel rejoiced when their captivity as a nation was turned—but you can rejoice before you ever see a turn-around or a change in your circumstances. Why? Because you serve the great "I Am" Who can turn any situation around for your good and His glory!

PSALM 126:1–3 (NIV)

1 When the Lord brought back the captives to Zion, we were like men who dreamed.
2 Our mouths were filled with laughter, our tongues with songs of joy. Then it was said among the nations, "The Lord has done great things for them."
3 The Lord has done great things for us, and we are filled with joy.

Notice it says in verse 2, *"Our mouths were filled with laughter, our tongues with songs of joy. THEN it was said among the nations, 'The Lord has done great things for them.'"* When the Israelites rejoiced in the Lord with laughter and songs of joy and praise, that was when others took notice that the Lord had done something for them. In the same way, if we want to see the manifestation of something we're believing for, we must rejoice and be glad in the Lord!

Let's read the rest of Psalm chapter 126.

PSALM 126:4–6 (NIV)

4 Restore our fortunes, O Lord, like streams in the Negev.
5 Those who sow in tears will reap with songs of joy.
6 He who goes out weeping, carrying seed to sow, will return with songs of joy, carrying sheaves with him.

You may start out sowing seeds of faith in God's Word while your heart is still breaking, your mind is dazed, and your whole world is turned upside down. But if you hold fast to your confession of faith and to an attitude of joy and rejoicing and take hold of the strength of God, you *will* reap your harvest, your promised blessing! With "songs of joy," you will return from the place of your brokenness, carrying your sheaves, your harvest, with you!

There is another truth we can glean from Psalm chapter 126. Verse 2 says, *"Our mouths were filled with laughter, our tongues with songs of joy"* (NIV). You've probably heard the expression, "Laughter is the best medicine." Medical research has proven that laughter helps the human body heal. When a person laughs, certain chemicals are released in the brain that actually speed up the body's healing process. So medical science understands that if a patient stays upbeat and positive, the person's chances for recovery improve. At the same time, a patient who's down and depressed diminishes his chances for improvement.

God already knew that! He created the human body, and He said, *"A MERRY HEART does good, like medicine, But a broken spirit dries the bones"* (Prov. 17:22). Other translations say, *"A REJOICING heart..."* (YLT) and *"A CHEERFUL heart..."* (NIV). Laughter really is like medicine!

It's Time to Look for the 'Son' Through the Storm Clouds

Whatever circumstance is trying to diminish your focus on God and His Word, remember that you don't have to bear the weight of it. You can take hold of the strength of the Lord and receive the ability to leap like a deer! You can rejoice that although things look bad today, the future is bright, and God's divine plan is coming to pass in your life.

No dark storm cloud can overcome the light of God's Word, and no circumstance or giant can overpower you when you're standing on the solid rock of the Word. It's time to look for the "Son" through the storm clouds of adversity. He is your constant companion, your peace in the midst of the storm, your strength, your salvation—and your anchor in rough waters! The future *is* bright with promise when you know you're not alone on the sea of life and that whatever storm is brewing on the horizon, God will see you safely through!

Why should you consider attending
RHEMA
Bible Training Center?

Here are a few good reasons:

- Training at one of the top Spirit-filled Bible schools anywhere
- Teaching based on steadfast faith in God's Word
- Growth in your spiritual walk coupled with practical training in effective ministry
- Specialization in the area of your choosing:
  Youth or Children's Ministry, Evangelism, Pastoral Care, Missions, or Supportive Ministry
- Optional intensive third-year programs—School of Worship, School of Pastoral Ministry, School of World Missions, and General Extended Studies
- Worldwide ministry opportunities—while you're in school
- An established network of churches and ministries around the world who depend on RHEMA to supply full-time staff and support ministers

Call today for information or application material.
1-888-28-FAITH (1-888-283-2484)
www.rbtc.org

RHEMA Bible Training Center admits students of any race, color, or ethnic origin.

OFFER CODE—BKORD:PRMDRBTC

Word Partner Club:

WORKING *together* TO REACH THE WORLD!

People. Power. Purpose.

Have you ever dropped a stone into water? Small waves rise up at the point of impact and travel in all directions. It's called a ripple effect. That's the kind of impact Christians are meant to have in this world—the kind of impact that the RHEMA family is producing in the earth today.

The *Word Partner Club* links Christians with a shared interest in reaching people with the Gospel and the message of faith in God.

Together we are reaching across generations, cultures, and nations to spread the Good News of Jesus Christ to every corner of the earth.

To join us in reaching the world, visit **www.rhema.org/wpc**
or call, 1-800-54-FAITH (543-2484)

Always on.

For the latest news and information on products,
media, podcasts, study resources, and
special offers, visit us online 24 hours a day.

Free Subscription!

Call now to receive a free subscription to *The Word of Faith* magazine from Kenneth Hagin Ministries. Receive encouragement and spiritual refreshment from . . .

- *Faith-building articles from Kenneth W. Hagin, Lynette Hagin, and others*
- *"Timeless Teaching" from the archives of Kenneth E. Hagin*
- *Feature articles on prayer and healing*
- *Testimonies of salvation, healing, and deliverance*
- *Children's activity page*
- *Updates on RHEMA Bible Training Center, RHEMA Bible Church, and other outreaches of Kenneth Hagin Ministries*

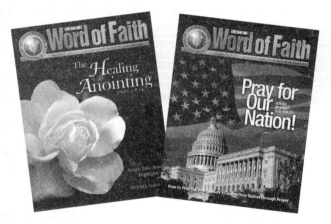

Subscribe today for your free *Word of Faith*!

1-888-28-FAITH (1-888-283-2484)

www.rhema.org/wof